LOVE AND WAR

A London Terrier's Tale of 1915–16

Compiled by
PETER TRAFFORD

This book is dedicated to the memory of my parents
Edward Henry (Ted) Trafford M.M.
27 November 1892 – 30 November 1972

and

Patience (Pat) Rose (née Randall)
15 May 1891 – 5 November 1964

Letters and an account of the 20th. Battalion, The County of London Regiment (Blackheath and Woolwich) T.F., during the early years of the Great War.

ACKNOWLEDGEMENTS

I am indebted to members of the staff of The Public Records Office, The Imperial War Museum, The National Army Museum and the Bristol central Library for their courteous help.

Officers of the Queen's Own Regimental Association have encouraged me in completing this work, and the Association's Bulletins have helped to clarify some historical points.

Mr. N. Bowyer has placed his considerable photographic skills at my disposal in producing good prints from old and faded photographs.

Mrs. B. Farrow and Mrs. M. Paul did sterling work in the initial typing of the letters.

The Imperial War Museum has kindly supplied two photographs; a number of cartoons by Captain Bruce Bairnsfather are included among the illustrations. They are taken from *Fragments from France* volumes 1–4 (1915–16).

My wife Josie, has been tolerant and understanding when, in my retirement I have immersed myself in the past and spent many hours poring over maps and letters.

Finally, my friends at Burleigh Press have been extremely helpful; without their enthusiasm and patient advice this book could not have appeared.

March 1992 PETER TRAFFORD

First Published 1992

This book is a tribute to All Ranks of the 20th. Battalion,
The County of London Regiment (Blackheath and Woolwich)
who embarked for the Western Front on 9 March 1915
and to all who served subsequently in the battalion
during the Great War.

ISBN 0 902780 10 7

Printed by Burleigh Press Ltd, Bristol BS2 0YA

INTRODUCTION

This book comprises the letters – every one of them – written by my father Ted Trafford, to my mother, then Patience Randall while he was serving in France with the 20th. (County of London) Battalion (Blackheath and Woolwich) between March 1915 and September 1916.

The letters speak for themselves; they have not been edited. Ted, as a good soldier, kept no diary and his letters give away no military secrets. To place them in context I have compiled a simple military narrative which month by month will give the reader some idea of the conditions under which the ordinary infantryman worked and played, fought, lived and sometimes died. No formal history of the 20th. London has ever been written.

Ted Trafford and Pat Randall had known each other from childhood, both[redacted] coming from police families who had lived in adjoining police quarters in the West End of London. Their fathers had retired from the Metropolitan Police as Inspectors in 1908.

Ted's home was 73 Arngask Road, Catford where he lived with his parents, sister Elsie and two younger brothers Stan and Harold. Elsie married Will Anderson in August 1914 and he and his brother Alec later enlisted in the London Scottish (14th. London Regiment). Ted and Stan were both members of Westcombe Park Rugby Football Club and had served two years as Territorials at the outbreak of war. Stan proceeded to a Commission in the 20th. in 1917, was awarded the Military Cross for an action at Bouchavesnes on 1 September 1918 and was seriously wounded. Harold, though under age, enlisted in the 20th. but was discharged as medically unfit after an attack of "Trench Foot".

Ted Trafford had been a choir-boy at All Souls Church, Langham Place and later attended Blackheath Road School in Greenwich. His schooling ended at fourteen but he followed evening classes in English, mathematics and book-keeping after starting work. In 1914 he was employed in the Land Valuation Office in Lewisham Hill and he was able to resume there after his demobilisation in 1919.

Later he became a part-time Collector of Taxes working from his home (96 Humber Road, Blackheath) and from an office which he rented two evenings per week at 203A Trafalgar Road, Greenwich. Eventually, in the 1930s he became an Established Civil Servant in the Inland Revenue Department from which he retired in 1954. His last post was as Chief Collector of Taxes, London 1 Area (Piccadilly).

Ted's love of cricket never left him; pre-1914 he played for the Ivanhoe C.C.; in the 1930s for the Inland Revenue C.C. at Grove Park and in the late '40s and early '50s for Ritchings Park C.C. at Iver. After his retirement to Somerset he played for the Wells City and Evercreech sides and later umpired many matches for these two clubs.

Pat Randall had completed her education at the City of London School, Blackfriars and matriculated at London University in 1908. She entered the Civil Service and was working in the Mount Pleasant Office of the G.P.O. in 1915–16. Her mother had died in 1909 and now she was also keeping house for her father and her brother Charlie. As recounted in letter No. 74, Charlie was wounded at Loos in 1915 returned to the Western Front in 1917, was posted to the 19th. London and wounded again and captured in April 1918.

Through the Randall side of her family Pat had cousins who are mentioned in some of the letters. Closest to Pat were Elsie Phillips who became an officer in the W.A.A.C. in 1917 and who married Will James of the 15th. London (Civil Service Rifles), and the family of Harry Rose, master boat builder of Maidenhead – Jack (Canadian Army), Nellie Gaskell and Effie Verhoeven, both of whom married United States citizens.

A colleague and close personal friend of Pat's was Evelyn Milliken and reference is made in some letters to visits to the Milliken family home at Pinner, Middlesex.

Pat and Ted Trafford on their Wedding Day – 6 January 1917.

Stan Trafford, 1916
20th. London.

Will Anderson, 1916
London Scottish.

Charlie Randall, 1915
20th. London.

Will Pike, 1918
London Irish Rifles.

Elsie Phillips (W.A.A.C) and
Will James (Civil Service Rifles)
on their Wedding Day, 3-10-17.

Jack Rose, 1917
Canadian Army.

"THE TWENTIETH"

The 20th. (County of London) Battalion, the London Regiment (Blackheath and Woolwich) T.F. came into being on 1 April 1908 when the 2nd. and 3rd. Volunteer Battalions of The Royal West Kent Regiment amalgamated. This date marked the end of the Volunteer Force and the beginning of the Territorial Force; the latter title was changed in 1921 to the Territorial Army. In 1920 the 20th. was granted an additional honour – the title of "The Queen's Own".

Investigation into the early ancestry of the 20th. reveals the existence of a volunteer unit formed to protect Greenwich Palace in 1543; the "Trained Bands and Auxiliary Forces of London" were inspected by Queen Elizabeth I in 1585 in what is now Greenwich Park. The Greenwich Unit was in action in 1643 at the Battle of Newbury. Royal Dockyard workers at Deptford formed a Foot Company of Volunteers in 1659 which became incorporated into the Deptford Company of the new Volunteer Force two hundred years later. A Blackheath Cavalry Unit was in existence from 1798 until 1909. The Loyal Greenwich Volunteer Infantry and the Loyal Greenwich Water Fencibles were both formed in 1803 and amalgamated in 1814 to survive until the creation of the Volunteer Force in 1859.

The life of the 20th. came to an end in 1935 when a reorganisation of the Home Defence Forces saw the battalion change into a Searchlight Regiment R.E.; but the cap badge and buttons (the White Horse of Kent) were retained and also the Regimental March "Wi' a Hundred Pipers". How that tune came to be adopted by the 20th. remains a mystery.

On its formation in 1908 the 20th. had inherited as its headquarters, Holly Hedge House on Blackheath. This fine Georgian brick house, once the property of the Earls of Dartmouth, had been the residence of the Vicars of Lewisham from 1804 until 1888. A number of alterations and additions had been made to the house over the years and the stables, coach house and other outbuildings had been adapted to military needs. Rooms in the Officers' Mess retained their Georgian panelling and the elegant wooden staircase of the original house survived. Sadly, the buildings were severely damaged by enemy action in 1943 and Regimental records of the first war were destroyed; the ruined remains of Holly Hedge House were demolished in 1947.

The Territorial Force had been established to provide a Home Defence Army to assist the small peace-time regular army and new legislation was required after the outbreak of war on 4 August 1914 to permit the deployment of Territorial Battalions overseas.

Holly Hedge House, Blackheath in the 1930s.
Front door – Officers' Mess.

The 20th. was one of four infantry battalions comprising the 5th. London Infantry Brigade; this with the 4th. and 6th. Brigades, plus artillery and supporting services (engineers, signals, ordnance, transport and medical) made up the 2nd. London Division. Divisional calvalry was lacking from the formation of the Territorial Force until 1915.

The 2nd. Division of the regular army comprising the 4th., 5th. and 6th. Brigades had been sent to France with the British Expeditionary Force in August 1914, and it soon became apparent that confusion would arise if the London Territorial soldiers used identical division and brigade numbers. The Territorial formations were therefore renumbered with effect from 11 May 1915 when the 20th. found itself part of 141 Brigade in the 47th. (London) Division. In June 1915, the 141st. Light Trench Mortar Battery was formed from personnel of the four infantry battalions constituting 141 Brigade, and in December of the same year – the 141st. Machine Gun Company.

Throughout this narrative, the new formation numbers will be used. The London Territorial Battalions making up the 47th. Division were:

140 Bde.	13th. London	The Kensingtons
	14th. London	The London Scottish
	15th. London	The Prince of Wales' Own Civil Service Rifles
	16th. London	The Queen's Westminster Rifles
141 Bde.	17th. London	The Poplar and Stepney Rifles
	18th. London	The London Irish
	19th. London	The St. Pancras
	20th. London	The Blackheath and Woolwich
142 Bde.	21st. London	The First Surrey Rifles
	22nd. London	The Queen's
	23rd. London	The Clapham
	24th. London	The Queen's (Kennington)

Recruiting for the 20th. had been satisfactory but the battalion was not at full strength at the outbreak of war; Ted Trafford had enlisted in 1912 as had other young men – particularly from the sports clubs of South East London. Well represented were the Rugby Football Clubs – Old Dunstonians, Westcombe Park, Charlton Park – the Ivanhoe Sports Club and Goldsmith's College. Stan Trafford and Charlie Randall had also enlisted in the 20th. before August 1914.

At the beginning of August 1914 the country had six regular infantry divisions abroad, stationed throughout the Empire, and six regular divisions plus 14 Territorial Divisions for Home Defence. The British Expeditionary Force, despatched to France within two weeks of the start of hostilities, was a small but well-equipped and well-trained army; almost inevitably, it soon suffered serious losses and three battalions of 140 Bde. were sent as reinforcements. The London Scottish crossed to the continent on 15 September 1914 and the Kensingtons and the Queen's Westminsters in early November. The first full Territorial Division sent to the Western Front was the 46th. (North Midlands) followed shortly afterwards in March 1915 by the 47th.

The London troops spent the autumn and winter of 1914–15 in Hertfordshire in intensive training, though hampered by very wet weather and shortage of equipment. The 20th., with the rest of 141 Bde., were billeted in and around Hatfield; the other two brigades were centred on St. Albans and Watford.

MARCH 1915

On Friday 5 March 1915 it became apparent to the troops that the 20th. was about to move. At 12.00 hours the usual week-end leaves had been authorised but these were all cancelled at 14.00 hours and two hours later arrangements had been made for the immediate recall of all men away from the battalion.

The battalion paraded in marching order at 05.00 hours on Tuesday 9 March under the Command of Col. E. J. Moore C.B., V.D., 31 officers, 1103 N.C.O.s and men, and 78 horses, with two machine guns and 21 wagons – and marched to Harpenden Station for entrainment. The trains arrived in Southampton Docks at about three o'clock in the afternoon; each half battalion was split into three parties for embarkation – one party to each of the three troop transports waiting at the quayside, thus ensuring a mix of all four battalions on each ship. The transports were *Viper*, *Queen Alexandra* and *Duchess of Argyll*, while a fourth ship *Trafford Hall*[1] carried the horses and the transport wagons.

The little convoy sailed during the dark hours and after an uneventful crossing, disembarkation at Le Havre began at 07.30 hours. As he came ashore each man was issued with a goat-skin coat, fur gloves and extra underwear. The 20th. marched off at 10.00 hours to Rest Camp no. 2 five miles away above Harfleur where they were lodged in tents for twenty-four hours: it was a very cold windy night with flurries of snow. At noon on 11 March the Battalion marched out of camp to the Gare des Marchandises, Le Havre where a 58 wagon train awaited them. The officers had a carriage which accommodated eight per compartment, though there were only six in that occupied by the Commanding Officer; other ranks were accommodated in horse/cattle wagons with approximately forty men in each.

A long slow journey followed; leaving Le Havre at 17.19 hours the train did not arrive in Cassell until 13.20 the following day. Then a further five mile march brought the troops to rather unsatisfactory billets in the village of Hardifort for a few days relaxation. That evening a horse was badly injured when, in the dark, a ration wagon was in collison with a motor-car opposite the Quartermaster's Stores at the cross-roads half a mile north-west of Hardifort village. A Church Parade was held on Sunday 14 March and the same day the soldiers received their first mail from home.

1 Ted Trafford sailed with the Transport Section in *Trafford Hall*, a ship of 5321 tons belonging to the Ellerman Line. The coincidence of the name of the ship must have been unknown to Ted or it would certainly have been mentioned at some time in the family. Presumably the ships' names had been painted out for security reasons.

Long marches through the reserve areas behind the front were to become a feature of life for the infantry; the 20th. left Hardifort on 18 March heading south through Cassell, then via Ste. Marie-Cappel and Hondequem to La Kreule on the northern outskirts of Hazebrouck where a convoy of London buses waited to take them on the next stage of their journey. Forty-two buses per battalion with 35–40 men per bus, carried them nineteen miles through Hazebrouck, St. Venant and Lillers to Allouagne where a few days of intensive training followed – particularly musketry practice on the ranges at Labeuvrière. The pit-head facilities at the coal mine in Auchel afforded welcome baths for the troops.

A Holy Communion Service was celebrated on 25 March and attended by 12 officers and 75 other ranks; three days later initiation and familiarisation visits to the firing line commenced. Small groups of officers and N.C.O.s were taken into the trenches between Béthune and La Bassée, where the line was held by regulars of the 4th. (Guards) Brigade alternating with the 6th Infantry Brigade, both of the 2nd. Division.

No. 1 **11.30 p.m. Monday 8 March 1915**

Just heard that we move off at 5 a.m. tomorrow. Charlie is coming with us. Will write at first opportunity.

Good-bye. Yours, Ted

No. 2 **3.30 p.m. Tuesday 9 March 1915**

Writing this on the boat at Southampton. Will write again when I get the opportunity.

Good-bye. Much love, Ted

P.S. I feel quite well.

No. 3 **13 March 1915**

My dear Pat,

We are now only a few miles from the firing line and can distinctly hear the heavy guns. My billet is a loft with straw for a bed. We arrived last night. The worst part was the journey from the coast to here. A journey lasting 22 hours. In our truck, in reality a horse box, we had 41 men. Charlie was in the next truck. He is in this company. The journey by sea was quite a tame affair. It was very calm. I came with our transport and some remounts. Hundreds of horses. It was great fun getting them up and down narrow gangways. We are now beginning to settle down but our travelling quite spoilt the food as we had to live on biscuits and bully beef. Not at all bad though, but a diet of which one soon tires. We look like getting a proper dinner today. We wash at the village pump and shave in the street – my mirror this morning being a cottage window. The weather is fine thank goodness. Stan and Charlie and I are quite well. Please let them have the news at home. I have not time or "papier" to write at present to them.

Good-bye for the present, my dear. Yours ever, Ted

No. 4 [Allouagne] 19 March 1915

We have now made another move and after a march and a long motor 'bus ride *on a Grove Park 'bus* we have arrived somewhere in . . . . I should have written earlier but I understand that letters would not be dispatched until we had reached our present destination. We are in a larger town but the billet we occupied last night was awful – a brewery loft with a stone floor, no windows but heaps of violent ventilation, no straw and no blankets. We reached our "nest" by means of an iron ladder. It was a fearfully cold night and this morning the whole place is liberally sprinkled with snow. We are hoping for a change today. We had one yesterday after out comfortable beds in the straw at the farmhouse we left. If you have knitted any more socks they will be welcome as the roads here are awful and have already made my feet a little sore, for which complaint clean socks are a good remedy. I can also, so far, obtain no English tobacco and French stuff is almost unsmokable. I do hope my dear, that you do not worry yourself too much. You must try not to do so. We have run no risks whatever yet, although we have, I believe, taken part in a big battle as supports who were not required. I am writing this in a café where I am breakfasting. I have drunk more coffee since I have been here than ever before.

Now dearest, you must understand that I cannot write too fully of our doings because of the censor, but he will I am sure, not prevent me assuring you of my constant love for you, so for the present a loving "au revoir".

Yours ever, Ted

No. 5 23 March 1915

Thanks so much for your last two letters which arrived on Sunday and Monday last. It is a good idea of yours to enclose writing paper. We have quite enough to carry and pack without a store of stationery. I am still billeted in the loft but we have now got straw on the floor and have blankets. On Saturday and Sunday last I was on guard at Divisional Headquarters and was awake all night. I caught a chill then I think, and went sick yesterday and although the doctor said I was to have a day off, I was forced to turn out as was everybody else to an inspection by Sir J. French. This took about five hours. I have got another day off today but feel better. It is nothing serious, so do not worry, although for a day or so I have felt queer. The doctor's instruction was to "stay in the warm and drink hot milk". Where either was to be found he did not say.

I have however found a farmhouse where I can get heaps of boiled milk, and I am taking full advantage. The weather which was very wintry at first has not improved altho' the nights are cold.

I am glad you write long letters – do not ever fear that you will bore me with their length. You must really forgive me not writing before.

Now my dear, you know I would like you, so much, to have a ring and you also know it is impossible for us, at present, to choose it together. If we did I should only be a looker-on. You would do all the choosing. Therefore you can surely do it alone, although I should so much like to be with you. As regards the cost, the figure you suggest as the least, is quite alright. Get one that you are quite satisfied with and I am sure I shall be so. It is a certainty that my arrears of army pay will more than cover that amount. Tell Dad that about £6 is my idea. If yours is more, then so is mine. You wonder what I look like in my fur coat. It is a black coat almost like bear-skin with one white and one fawn sleeve. You must imagine the rest. It is very warm but also heavy when carried rolled up on one's back.

Please do not worry dearest. I will write and let you know of a move immediately. I think constantly of my girlie and the thought of her being uneasy and worrying about me is all that pains me.

"Au revoir". With all my love,

Yours ever, Ted

P.S. We have just been issued with cigarettes and tobacco – English too!

No. 6 — 25 March 1915

Thanks so much for your letter of Sunday last which reached me yesterday. I presume and sincerely hope that you are quite well. You did not say. I am pleased to say that I am much better today. I was able to smoke again today. A luxury I have had to forego since Sunday on account of my throat. It is a beastly wet day and there is mud everywhere. The whole country hereabouts including roads would make an admirable huge pigsty in its present condition. We got a bit wet this morning but are drying again. I am writing this in the brewery boiler house where it is at least warm and dry if very dirty. Did I tell you the loft we are in was in a brewery?

We are at present "standing by" already for a move at a moment's notice but I will let you know if we make a move. I am afraid my watch will not be much use much longer as I have smashed the glass and cannot get another to fit. I thought as you did, my dear, of the Sunday a month ago. It was a happy day "nil desperandum" there are happy days to come when all this is over, and then dearest, how much will we be to each other. More dear than if we had never parted. I know just how you felt when we said good-bye and how I felt but it is some consolation to know that the sacrifice, more on your side than mine, was for a good cause.

Thanks for the little calendar and for your promise to write so frequently. Your letters are so much to me.

Now dearest, good-bye for a little while. Keep as cheerful as you can. I am, with fondest love,

Ever yours, Ted

P.S. Some Formalin tablets and other medicines in tablet form would be very useful. They may be sending some from home, though.

No. 7 **27 March 1915**

Thanks so much for your letter and parcel. The whole of its contents were very welcome. I have now a good stock of tobacco as we get an ounce served out about every other day and Dad said in a letter that he was sending some as well.

Yesterday was a red letter day. The whole battalion had a bath. There are some mines a few miles off and there is a fine arrangement there, presumably for the workers, for bathing. Lots of hot shower baths. It was a treat, ever so much better than a tub in the yard. In the afternoon we had a washing day for our clothes, socks etc. It is a fine day here today, very bright and cold, but with heaps of mud still about. I do not think my boots will ever be quite dry. They make one's feet quite cold in the morning when they are put on.

We are trench digging today, and I am writing this out in the fields which are, just here, almost under water. There seems to be no drainage in these parts and the country is as flat as a saucer, in fact it is just like a series of huge saucers. Bleak, barren and slushy. Our sleeping place is the same but much more comfortable with straw and blankets. It was a cold night last night but I slept warmly. My cold has not left me although it is a lot better.

LATER

Returned now from our labour and I am finishing this in a café. Out to lunch today but in a place not quite up to Slater's. There was an aeroplane not far from here this morning and one could see the shells from the Allies' guns bursting around it.

I personally did not see them, nor did I see an air duel almost overhead on Sunday morning last, but I got graphic descriptions from eye-witnesses.

Have you got the ring? You know how much I should have liked to give it to you myself but you must content yourself with its significance. You may know that you are constantly in my thoughts, and it is impossible to put adequately in a letter an expression of my love for you. The more I think, the more I love. Try and take consolation in that and for the present "au revoir". With all my love,

Yours, Ted

P.S. I forgot to say, the vaseline bottle was smashed in the post and useless.

No. 8 **30 March 1915**

I received your letter of Friday last, yesterday. I am surprised that you had not at the time of writing received more letters from me. You have, I expect by now got the letters I have written. I have not yet been in the trenches although some of our battalion have been actually in the firing trenches. Luckily without casualities. I am now in a newly formed grenadier company and am being trained in the making and throwing of bombs, grenades etc. It is very interesting. I have had quite an easy day today but am making up for it with a night on guard. The nights are still intensely cold and we cannot seem to sleep warmly. I went out to tea at a little shop with Charlie yesterday. We had quite a merry little time. Tea is practically unknown in these parts. "Café au lait" very often without the "lait" is the substitute, but we got some excellent chocolate. Today at tea-time I went out with Leo and Stan to a farmhouse and regaled ourselves on eggs and milk. My cold is improving but my throat gets sore at nights. I have seen the Kentish Mercury and wish our present conditions were as bright as they are painted therein. I had a parcel from home yesterday. Tobacco is very flush, and I think I am being served out with more tomorrow.

I hope you will read this alright but I am writing under somewhat trying "circs" with only a candle for light. I am keenly waiting to hear again from you. I welcome your letters more than anything else.

Goodnight, dearest, I think always of you and wonder how you are getting on. I will write again very soon.

With heaps of love, Yours, Ted

P.S. Has my watch reached you yet?

Pat and Ted, March 1915.

APRIL 1915

On 7 April the battalion moved nearer to the front, marching via Chocques to Béthune to be billeted in the École des Jeunes Filles and to work for a week with the Berkshire Regiment (6 Bde.).

'A' and 'B' Companies of the 20th. were the first to take over full front line duties. On 14 April, 'B' Company, temporarily under the command of Major Matthews, took over sector A2 in front of Cuinchy, with 'A' Company in support and Battalion HQ in the Cuinchy support post. The next morning at 03.15 hours there was a stand-to for the explosion of mine no. 3 at 03.30, which also caused a German mine to go up prematurely. There was immediate heavy rifle fire but no other development; casualties for the first week in front line action were only 9 wounded. The battalion reassembled back in Béthune where a Church Parade was held in the theatre on Sunday 18 April.

A few days back in billets in Lapugnoy followed where news was received of the arrival of 'C' Squadron, King Edward's Horse (an Indian Regiment) as divisional cavalry. Lieutenants Honeybourne and Escombe were gazetted Captains with effect from 1 March. With increasing activity on the divisional front east of Festubert and Givenchy, the 20th. marched up to Gorre on St. George's Day but found the available accommodation extremely crowded. 'C' and 'D' Companies slept in railway wagons to avoid the worst of a very wet night. The next week was spent playing "Box and Cox" with the London Irish Rifles in manning the trenches in front of Festubert. Numbers were depleted by an outbreak of measles and the rest billets were within artillery range of the enemy. The marshy nature of the ground made the maintenance of trenches exceedingly difficult and on the left it was virtually impossible. Here sandbag breastworks marked the line and came to be known as the "grouse butts". Numerous dead had been buried by the Germans in shallow graves and the stench added to the unpleasantness of front line duties. The 20th. was now in four companies commanded by:

'A' Company Captain Hooper
'B' Company Captain Marchant
'C' Company Captain Ball
'D' Company Captain Dolphin

Two companies were in the first line with two in support. A great deal of heavy work was necessary at night in carrying up supplies of every sort as movement in daylight was impossible. The Battalion HQ remained in the rear of Festubert while the Battalion 2 i/c was given a separate command on the left (north) with his HQ at Brewery Pool, Rue à Cailloux.

No. 9 **2 April 1915**

Dearest Girlie,

Thanks so much for your last two letters. The last, with the welcome news has just arrived. I am very pleased that you are so well and satisfied. I only have one regret and that is that I could not be with you when you put it on for the first time. You know, however, that I would have been if I had not been so suddenly called up. I am delighted that you are well and especially so, now that you are happy in having a very sacred and continuous reminder of what we each are to the other. I hold you always first in my thoughts and you must know that you completely have all my love.

Things here are very monotonous at present. We hear occasionally a very heavy bombardment in the direction of the firing line. I am much better and except for a little throatiness at nights I am quite better. I do not now sleep on a stone floor but am very comfortable with straw in a wagon in a cartshed.

Stan and Leo are quite well and send kindest regards. I have been out to tea with them and Charlie today. I am glad you had such a jolly week-end. Today is Good Friday and I cannot help thinking of last Good Friday and at the same time looking forward to the next and the succeeding ones when we shall again be together.

Once again dearest, good-bye, with heaps of love, Ever yours, Ted

P.S. Today here is no different to any other.

No. 10 **4 April 1915**

I am expecting another letter from you today but the post is not yet in. Oh how eagerly I wait for your letters. They are to me like an oasis in the desert is to a traveller.

Today is Easter Sunday and we are having a thorough rest. We had an open air Church Service this morning. Our chaplain is a fine fellow. It was a good service and the singing of the old church Easter hymns reminded me of previous Easters spent with my girlie. Of course one could not help feeling the difference and wondering what she was doing and how she was spending her Easter, but I am afraid I am an optimist and I got a certain amount of comfort in looking forward to next and in fact all future Easters in her delightful company. I hope dearest, that you also will derive some satisfaction from the thought and that you will not be too unhappy this Easter. After the church parade we have no more parades today and I took the opportunity to go out to dinner at a neighbouring cafe. I had quite a good meal – pork and baked potatoes, some "vin blanc" and bread, butter and jam.

Yesterday was a perfect soaker. It rained all day. We had an inspection by General Haig (I believe) in the afternoon.

Has my watch arrived yet? I sent it off a week ago. Thanks for your promise of a parcel. Do not send too much at once or I shall find difficulty in storing.

You will be pleased to hear I am fit again. My cold has practically gone – I hope for good. There are no signs at present of an immediate move from here, although I expect we shall not stay very much longer. We are having a longer stay than troops here before us.

I hope you are keeping quite well. I have several letters to write today in answer to ones I have received from Mallet, Harry Sanders, your Dad and Will Anderson. I also have some sewing to do so you must excuse more for the present.

With fondest love, Ever yours, Ted

No. 11 [Annequin] **11 April 1915**

I hope you will not think it is my fault that you have not heard from me for some days, but we have made a move and while on the move we cannot send off letters. We are now at . . . ., and our company was the first to have a spell in the trenches and I could not write until we got back here to rest. We slept in a village before and after going up to the firing line which was shelled more or less the whole time. We had one casualty there and a few in the trenches. I expect that you have heard by this post that Charlie is quite alright. Stan is up there today. After a few minutes under fire one feels quite safe and everything goes on as if there were no Germans in the world. I slept quite comfortably while not on duty, in a dug-out with a sergeant of the Royal Berks. The firing quite failed to disturb my slumber. We were at that part of the line where our guards have made themselves so notorious and where O'Leary won his V.C.[1] We cooked our breakfast bacon and made tea, oxo etc. over little braziers made with empty tins. The whole thing was a novel experience and just as I had imagined it would be. It was a bit cold at night and on Friday morning while we were in there we had a sharp blizzard of snow and hail. The regulars who were with us seemed quite pleased with our fellows' coolness and general behaviour in the circumstances. Thanks very much for the parcel. Please don't send any more tobacco until I ask for some. I received yesterday a tin of chocolate from the fellows at the office. Ever such a lot. I do not know what I shall do with it if we move off in a hurry.

I hope you are quite well. I am perfectly fit. We had a game of Rugger yesterday but had to finish up prematurely as one fellow got his shirt torn off, another his braces and an officer ruined a fine cardigan; being so placed that things like that are not very easily replaced, we knocked off. There is a heavy artillery duel now on, and rumour has it that there has been more shelling this week than for months.

Au revoir, my dear.

With all my love, Yours ever, Ted

Footnote to No. 11:

1 Sgt. Michael O'Leary of the Irish Guards was awarded the Victoria Cross for his exploits at Cuinchy on 1 February 1915.

No. 12 — 14 April 1915

This green envelope is a new idea and a very fine one. It gives one an opportunity of writing without anyone in one's own battalion reading the letter. Also with these letters it doesn't matter how much one writes. You, must however, excuse the length of this as we have to leave here in an hour's time to take another turn in the trenches. Stan and Charlie are coming with us. We do not know how long we are off for, so if you don't hear for a day or two, don't worry darling. I will send you off a card at least at the first opportunity. I am so glad that we are engaged and I can assure you my dear of my constant love and affection. You are always in my thoughts and it is only for your sake that I have the slightest fear. I do not mind being out here for my own part, in fact there is a certain amount of fascination in the element of danger, but I always have the thought with me that for your sake I must take every precaution. How it pleased me to read in your letter "I know we love each other all the time". I know also that we do and the thought brings comfort and consolation. I shall think of that tonight when I am watching the German fireworks and listening for anything alarming.

I look forward as eagerly as you do, my dear, to the day when I come back to my girlie and when I can have you always and to know you are mine for ever.

I have several little jobs to do before we leave so once again, a loving au revoir.

Yours ever, Ted

No. 13 — 16 April 1915

I have been lucky to receive so many letters from you lately. I received your letter of Sunday about five minutes after I wrote my last letter and your Tuesday letter today. We came out of the trenches last evening and my sleep last night was the soundest I have ever had. We had 24 hours in the firing line, heaps of excitement and a good march up and down, without a wink of sleep so you may guess the absence of a bed did not matter a little bit. We were about 50 or 60 yards from the German line and were "standing to" more or less all night. The Royal Engineers completed a mine under the Germans and at 3 o'clock yesterday morning they fired it. I have never seen such a sight. It was very impressive and awful. As soon as it went up we opened rapid fire and simply poured bullets into them for about twenty minutes. The explosion was just a huge blinding flash with an awful roar. Our parapet of sand-bags rocked and in one place came down and injured two of our company. One of the worst tragedies was that our "grub bag" got buried. The bread was smashed to crumbs and jam tins and café au lait were all smashed and mixed up. During the night I and two other volunteers went out to find out what the enemy were doing and we were about 30 yards from the Germans and some of them were out putting up wire entanglements. Charlie was working on the mine for a good part of the night.

I am quite well and I hope you are also, my dear.

Rather amusing about "Grace's soldier" isn't it?

I have forgotten to tell you that my platoon is now no. 8 and has been for some weeks. It may interest you to know that Bob Hapgood is in my section.

Now my dear, good night. The others are all turning in so I think I will. Kindest regards from Leo and Stan.

With all my love, Ever yours, Ted

Footnote to No. 13:
"Leo" was Leo Shurly, a member of the Ivanhoe Cricket Club, who had enjoyed river outings with Ted and Pat at Maidenhead. Killed at Loos in September 1915.

No. 14 [Béthune] 18 April 1915

Another Sunday has come round. Today is a grand spring day. I should just enjoy a 'bus ride to say Farnborough, this morning. It would be a nice change after taking all my recent exercise in the form of walking. We had a concert last evening arranged by the Staffordshires who are also in the town. The London Scots are quite near here but I have not yet seen any of them I know. I am soon going out to look for Will James and Will Pike, both their battalions are in the town. There is a nice theatre here where the concert was held and where we had our Church Parade this morning. It seemed very strange to have a service with stage scenery behind the chaplain.

I wonder how you are spending your Sunday my dear? I know you wish as much as I do that we could spend it together, but we must wait with what patience we can command, just a bit longer and then let us hope for a long and happy future.

I have discovered what your French phrase is. *We do!*

Stan and Leo send kind regards. They are both well. Please give mine to your Dad and Miss Guymer.

Au revoir, dearest. With heaps of love, Ted

No. 15 [Lapugnoy] 20 April 1915

I did not get another letter today as I expected. Yours usually reach me at least every other day. I know, however, that you have not forgotten me so I look forward eagerly to tomorrow's post.

You will not perhaps hear from Charlie for a day or two as his platoon is isolated on account of an outbreak of fever. He is quite fit. I saw him playing footer this morning. We have had a long day today 5.30 to 4.30 except for mealtimes.

We have made another move. We are here, presumably for training, for a few days. My platoon is billeted in an empty theatre. I sleep on the stage. I have had some funny billets – a farm shed, a brewery, a cart, a school and now a theatre.

The scenery around here is quite pretty and easily the best we have seen in France. It is only a small place and the theatre is quite small. There are some refugees also in the back part of the building. We came here yesterday. It was a very hot day yesterday, quite summery, but today was colder. We wash in a stream which runs thro' the grounds of a wrecked chateau. We have a good deal of fun. Our latest is to play soccer with a rugger ball, and to act impromptu dramas on our bedroom floor.

We were in the trenches 24 hrs. on each occasion. I am quite well and I hope you are also. I trust you have got rid of that tired feeling.

Leo and Stan send kind regards. Now my dear, a loving good night.

Ever yours, Ted

P.S. I found Will James on Sunday. He sends kindest regards. I found Will Pike's billet but he had gone to hospital with measles.

No. 16 — 23 April 1915

Thanks so very much for your letters and parcel received yesterday. You send a fine selection. The butter was welcome and the paste a great luxury. I shared the tinned fruit amongst a few and we all enjoyed it. It was a good idea to put soap and formalin tablets in, but my previous stock of both articles was not exhausted. The whole collection was both useful and pleasing. You are very thoughtful and I expect you have nearly as much pleasure in packing it as I have in receiving it. If you do, you get a good deal.

We are moving from here tomorrow for another turn in the trenches. This time, I think, for four days. Do not worry, my dear, I am quite fit and I will not, for your dear sake, take *unnecessary* risks.

The little French book you sent is jolly good. Didn't you think so?

Charlie is still in quarantine so I have not seen him for a day or two. Stan and I went out to tea tonight and I saw Leo yesterday.

We were all turned out of our billet last night and we had a battalion concert in here. It was quite good. Yesterday morning we had a jolly fine bath at a coal mine some 3 or 4 miles distant. Another luxury!

Now my dear, I hope you are quite well. I think so much about you. The only thing that I have to worry me at all is that you must be miserable. It is my only fear that the people at home are upset.

Oh how I yearn for you, my girlie! I just long to feel your cool hands round my neck and to be holding you tight for a big good-night kiss.

Good-night darling, the boards and blanket are inviting me to sleep.

Much love, Yours ever, Ted

No. 17 [Gorre] **25 April 1915**

We have made another move now and are in a village which is within range of the German guns. We arrived here yesterday afternoon while the place was being shelled. Our billet is in a loft and we are fairly comfortable when compared with some of our chaps who had to sleep in the open. Our roof let the rain in a little but we bunged the holes up with tin etc. and so kept a bit dry.

We are resting today; not even a church parade, and have to be ready to move off up to the trenches tonight.

A German spy has just been captured here and marched thro' the village. The guns have started again.

There is really nothing else to write about but I will write and tell you all about it when we come out.

I have had a letter from Harry Sanders and Les Howard this week and from my Aunt Lucy but her parcel has not yet turned up.

Letters are now being collected so good-bye for the present, dearest.

With all my love, Ted

No. 18 [Cuinchy] **28 April 1915**

Your letter of Sunday has just reached me. We are resting after two days under fire. We went into the firing line at a ruined village. I have never seen such a scene of desolation as that wrecked place. Every house was damaged and most were absolutely knocked to pieces. The road was covered with huge cavities caused by the shells and even the churchyard was ploughed up. The Church was wrecked, the roof gone completely, except for a large crucifix which stands intact. Your cocoa cubes were very useful, for a drink of hot cocoa warms one up when the night is cold. The days are warm – today is quite summery, and Charlie and I have just been swimming in the canal here. It was a great treat to get all our clothes off and enjoy the water and a sun bath.

You wonder if I have changed. I am not much different in appearance except that my hair is cropped like a convict's and I think when I return to civilization that my manners and general demeanour will return to normal.

One thing remains unchanged and that, my dear, is my love for you.

I am pleased you had a nice time at Pinner. I expect you have received my green envelope by now.

We seem to have started a system of two days in and two days rest so we shall be off again tomorrow.

Au revoir, my dear. Yours ever, Ted

MAY 1915

On 3 May the 20th. marched out via Gorre, Essars and Béthune to mostly familiar billets round Lapugnoy. Battalion HQ was established in a house said to have been occupied by the British in 1815 after Waterloo. The following day Captain Marchant was found shot in his room and he was buried in the château grounds at Gorre. The renumbering of the brigades and division already referred to, became effective on 11 May.

The battalion spent a week in support of the divisional front, being kept on the move in anticipation of being required at short notice in various sectors. On 10 May they marched to Les Façons behind the L'Épinette sector north of Festubert where billets were available in two farms for some of the troops, the remainder having to bivouac in the open. The next day came another move – to La Couture and a second night in bivouac. They were pulled back to Béthune on the 13 May and billeted in the theatre and surrounding buildings, only to move again the following day to Le Préol ready to go up into the Givenchy sector which was to be held "at all costs" in the face of mounting offensive action by the Germans. On 14 May Ted Trafford was detached from the 20th. to join the cadre of 141 Trench Mortar Battery then newly formed. His letters reveal that the trench mortars were in constant demand by whichever battalion was holding the 141 Brigade front, so that personnel did not have the advantage of the alternating short spells of front line and reserve duties enjoyed by the rifle battalions. 141 T.M.B. suffered casualties on 16 May when one of their mortars exploded killing three and wounding four men. The dead were buried in a garden 30 yards west of the Post Office at Givenchy – Pont Fixe.

The 20th. took over Sidbury trench on 18 May, which was very wet and uncomfortable being little more than a glorified ditch; they were withdrawn into billets in Harley Street after twenty-four hours but the following morning found them again in front of Givenchy in sector B2 with 'C' and 'D' Coys. in the firing line, 'B' Coy. holding the Marie Redoubt and Gunner Siding, and 'A' Coy. in reserve in dug-outs immediately to the rear of Harley Street. The London front was heavily shelled from 16–19 May in retaliation for a largely unsuccessful attack by the First Army north of Festubert on the left of the 47th Division. In a brief respite on 24 May the 20th. enjoyed the luxury of bathing in the La Bassée Canal but the following evening they were hurried back to the front line to reinforce 142 Bde. which had suffered heavy casualties in an attack on the German S-bend north-east of Givenchy and in subsequent desperate efforts to retain the captured front-line positions. For four days the 20th. fought alongside the 24th. Battalion losing twenty-three men killed and missing and one officer and forty-four other ranks wounded, before coming out of the line to rest in billets at Le Préol. The respite here was short-lived as the billets came under light shell-fire on both 30 and 31 May. During this period, Ted Trafford was with the 17th London in an exposed position in front of Cuinchy on the canal bank near the Pont Fixe.

Brigadier General Nugent was killed by a stray bullet on 31 May and was succeeded as commander of 141 Bde. by Lieut. Colonel Thwaites whose promotion was announced two days later.

No. 19 **2 May 1915**

Dearest Girlie,

Thanks for your two letters. The one you wrote on Tuesday night was brought to me in the trenches and I received Thursday's this morning. The "trenches" are not dug out except very shallow and the necessary protection is made with a breastwork of sandbags, hurdles and earth. The ground is too marshy to dig more than a foot or two. In fact the position is on a marsh. We completed another two days up there last night and slept in this loft until nearly dinner-time today. We had quite a nice time except for sniping and some firing during the night. We were shelled a bit but without much damage. There was a terrific bombardment a little farther up the line early yesterday morning. I have never seen such a sight or heard such a noise. We are back here now for either two or four days rest, after which we go up for either two or four. You mention the new shells which the Huns are using. They are, in my opinion, absolutely diabolical inventions, but our people have quickly found an antidote and we, while in the firing line, are issued with muzzles of wire covered with cloth which are soaked in some special liquid, a supply of which is placed at intervals along the line, and then fastened over the nose and mouth.

It is not warm enough to swim today but we have had hot tubs in the yard.

I am quite fit as are Stan, Charlie and Leo. There is nothing more of import to write about except that in your next parcel a few Saccarine (? spelling) tablets would be most acceptable. It was jolly nice to get your letter yesterday, more so as I was not expecting it up there. Bob Hapgood and I shared a dugout or shelter and we had a nice chat about home and all sorts of nice things during the night, while we snatched a little rest in between watching, listening, firing, repairing parapets and filling sandbags, etc.

I know, my dear, that you cannot help wondering and worrying a little, but I know you are a brave little girlie so keep your "pecker" up. We are all cheerful here – in fact we even sing to the Germans!

When you next write remember me to Nellie. Kindest regards to your Dad.

Au revoir, dearest. Yours ever, Ted

No. 20 5 May 1915

Since replying to your last letter I expect another has arrived our here for me but I have been away from the battalion since Monday morning so I have not yet received it. I am at the R.A.M.C. station. I came here because a stitch in my leg which was left in had worked to the surface and had to be extracted. I am kept here to rest my leg while the tiny puncture heals – a matter of another day or so – when I shall rejoin the battn. which is now back from the line for a period. I walk about and am not in the least inconvenienced.

I really cannot see why they keep me here, but a day or two of complete rest will not hurt me. I expected to go back to the battn. but I think now it will be tomorrow. I will send a PC as soon as I get out of here and write at the first opportunity. My letters should have been sent on to me but they haven't. I should have written about this before but I thought I should not have been kept here and I should not have more than incidentally mentioned the matter.

We sleep on spare stretchers here. They are more comfortable than the floor.

There is nothing more to say about anything so I will just tell you how I long for this war to end so that my girlie can become really mine.

With heaps of love, Yours ever, Ted

No. 21 7 May 1915

I am now back with the battalion and am feeling perfectly fit. We do not know when or what our next move will be. Thanks very much for the parcel. It was awaiting me when I got here last evening together with a parcel from the office, containing chocolate and a couple of new pipes. The respirators are very useful but we are simply inundated with them – each man possessing about three at least – from various donors. We are now to be attached to a regular division, where, at present we do not know.

We have been served out with long waterproof capes and our overcoats have been called in. This will make our packs a bit lighter but we shall miss our coats if we sleep in the open, and we carry extra ammunition to make up for the weight.

Do not think that I am ungrateful but please do not send out anything other than eatables unless I write for them. The towel you sent me for instance was really not required as the one I had was in quite good condition. I am using the new one and I soon found a home for the other one in someone else's kit. The toothbrush I had was also in good condition. Stan had the bootlaces as I have two pairs still in reserve. The tinned fruit, butter and paste was however highly appreciated and I thank you very much for sending all you did. A card of bachelor buttons would be very useful next time.

I have not received a letter from you for four days. You do not know how long that four days has seemed. I suppose it or they, have been sent on to me but did not arrive until I was back here. I do hope there is one in the post today. Your letters do buck me up. Just to know that there is the one little girlie in all the world who cares, who wonders what I am doing and who longs as I do for the happy day when we can again be together.

I do hope you are keeping quite well, dear, and that all is well with you.

Please thank your Dad for his lime juice tablets and give him my very kindest regards.

Now dear, I will close with heaps of love and au revoir.

Yours ever, Ted

No. 22 — 11 May 1915

I am writing this altho' I do not know whether I shall be able to send it off today. Our posts in and out have been very irregular of late. I did, however, get your Thursday's letter on Sunday.

We are out 'on trek' – supports just behind the firing line – and at present are in the prettiest little orchard you could imagine. We slept here last night. It is necessary to be in a place with trees so that the 'planes cannot spot us as we are within range of the enemy's guns. On Saturday night we marched nearly all night and then bivouacked in another orchard. We moved again on Sunday night and on this occasion slept on the floor of a farmhouse kitchen. The days are as hot as midsummer but the majority of us find it cold at night. I find I sleep well despite that. It is necessary to get up and stamp about once during the night, just to buck the circulation up. We have been unable to wash until this morning on account of the water being husbanded so carefully in case it was wanted for other purposes. We are bathing in biscuit tins today and I can assure you we look on that as a luxury.

I see on my little calendar and you also remind me in your letter, that next Saturday is your birthday. Well my dear, I wish you many happy returns of the date. I will not wish you returns of the day. By your next birthday let us hope the war will be ended. Today's weather reminds me very much of the days we have spent at Maidenhead and other nice places, together, and it is thoughts like that which make one long for home, but we have a little more to do out here before that longing can be satisfied and then the satisfaction will be all the sweeter. I think of you, my dear, all the time and when I lay down to sleep I wonder, oh so much, if you will sleep as well as I do. I expect you, even with a comfortable bed, find sleep rather elusive while I laying down with equipment and boots etc. all on, as we have to, after just a little while spent in thought sleep as sound as a top with the guns' boom as a lullaby.

This is all very rambling but I feel as if I must say something and what I would like to tell you as to where we are and what part we are taking etc. etc. is not allowed.

Once again then darling, au revoir.

With all my love, Yours, Ted

No. 23 — 13 May 1915

Thanks for your Sunday letter which arrived yesterday. There is really such a little to put in the letters in the way of actual news that I shall have to write a short letter. Thank your Dad for his letter and give him my kindest regards. Charlie is still quite well. We were relieved yesterday and are back in quite a large town again. After days on biscuits and bully beef it was a great pleasure to go out as we did last night – Stan and I – and have a good course dinner at a restaurant.

The "Lusitania" business has come as a shock to us all. It is a terrible affair to kill in cold blood so many people.

Do not be unnecessarily alarmed about us being near the Germans. The fact that we can shout to them does not mean we must put our heads out of the trench.

I am quite fit and well. We are in a theatre again for a billet – not the one we were in before. Stan's company is downstairs and he comes up to sleep with me on the floor of a little cloakroom. We were quite comfy in there last night, but have still to sleep in our clothes as we have no blankets or overcoats, until the winter comes round again and by that time I hope I shall not be in need of either, but that I shall again be monarch of a very small room at the rear of no. 73.

I have had such a nice lot of letters from you lately. It is nice to get a letter nearly every day although I cannot write one in reply each day. I am so lucky to have someone who writes such charming letters, and to have someone to love and who loves in return. Although we may be separated by what seems a huge distance we both have the great consolation that we are as one in thought. I am just burning to see you again. I often try to imagine my return which I hope will not be, now too far distant.

Until that happy day, au revoir, beloved.

Yours ever, Ted

Footnote to No. 23:
The trans-Atlantic liner "Lusitania" was torpedoed and sunk by a U-boat off the south-west coast of Ireland on 7 May 1915.

No. 24 — 18 May 1915

141 Trench Mortar Battery

You will be surprised to get a letter from me, written in a despondent mood, but I am afraid this one will be. I am writing this in the trenches under fire where I have been for four days and likely to stay until the brigade are relieved, when I cannot estimate. It is not this that upsets me, but the fact that I have been transferred from my battalion and am now attached to the above battery, in the same brigade, however. I am now away from all my pals, just because I happen to know how to work these mortars. I have just been called out of my dug-out to go and send over a few souvenirs so I shall have to finish this tomorrow. Good night, dear.

Wednesday morning, I think. It is still raining as it has been more or less for the past two days. I am in as muddy a state as I was sometimes on a very wet Saturday afternoon. The slush is over our boot tops. My feet have been soaked for three days. I have spent a fairly comfortable night in a hole, like a fox, only getting up twice to do a little bombarding. Will you please let mother have the news and my new address as I cannot at present send off a letter, except in a green envelope and I have but one.

Our job here is to discharge large bombs from a primitive kind of gun, and is quite interesting, although I wish I were back with the 20th.

I have had no letters for nearly a week and feel a bit "fed up". I expect it will soon wear off though and I shall soon be at home with my new comrades. The officer seems a fine chap.

It has also upset me to think that you are perhaps worrying what has become of me on account of the stoppage in my letters. I do so hope that this letter will set your fears at rest. Now, my dear, I shall soon have to close as we must get on with the anarchists' job again. Don't worry too much and please let my dear little mother hear about me as soon as possible. I have sent her a field service card. We are just getting shelled again, but I still think of my dear girlie and wish to be at her side. Au revoir, my beloved.

Yours ever, Ted

A Matter of Moment.
"What was that Bill?"
"Trench mortar."
"Ours or theirs?"

The Innocent Abroad.
Out since Mons: "Well, what sort of a night 'ave yer 'ad?"
Novice (but persistent optimist): "Oh, alright. 'Ad to get out and rest a bit now and again."

See Letter No. 24 From *Fragments from France* – Bruce Bairnsfather.

No. 25 — Whit-Sunday 23 May 1915

I must write today, altho' I do not think I have missed an opportunity. Of course, I suppose that you are remembering with me, previous Whitsuns. How I wish we could repeat some of them. I am still in the firing line, this being my ninth day.

I got your parcel this morning. It was very welcome. I went along the line during a lull and saw Stan and Charlie and Leo. All three are well. I think this is their fourth day in the trenches. When I opened the cigarettes in your parcel I found the enclosed. What irony? When I first saw that, I was dirty from head to foot and had not washed or shaved for eight days. I have since. What memories and pictures this little slip of paper conjures up? It is today an ideal summer's day, but of course the ideal is smashed here by the shriek and crash of shells, but the weather is grand. The trenches are getting dry again after a terrific thunderstorm last night. The artillery and thunder and lightning combined made the night hideous. I hope we are soon relieved for at least a short rest. I have already made a good start on your parcel. I breakfasted on some of the butter and lobster paste on biscuits – no bread in here now, only army biscuits – followed by fruit salad and "digestive" biscuits, the whole was washed down by smoky tea and your condensed milk, made delicious with saccharine.

I was quite an aristocrat to get such a meal here

The beans went well with the no. 1 Army Ration – a tin of preserved stew which needs only warming – at dinner time. The piece of cake went first of all when I opened the parcel. The tin you packed it all in will make a topping brazier. It is nearly tea-time and I shall again appreciate some of your gifts. The usual shelling is now in progress.

I hope you have received the cards I have posted. I think constantly of you, my beloved, and just long for your presence. Au revoir dear.

With all my love, Ever yours, Ted

Footnote to No. 25:
The enclosure referred to is a coupon measuring 2½″ × 1¾″ bearing on one side a rural picnic scene. The other side states that this is no. 3 in a series of 25 and that a full sized picture may be obtained from "De Reszke" Cigarettes in exchange for the top of a cigarette box plus a 2d. stamp.

No. 26 — 25 May 1915

I have received your letter of the 16th. I got it two days ago. We are still in the trenches, this being my eleventh day. Some of the men in my battalion have suffered with nerves but I am glad to say I am quite fit. The weather is splendid – far too good to spend out here when the river and the English country and seaside must be just lovely. I cannot write a long letter, but thought you would be pleased to get just a line or two. Au revoir, my dear.

With heaps of love, Yours ever, Ted

No. 27 27 May 1915 (but postmarked 26 May)

I was in luck this morning when your two letters of the 20th and 23rd arrived with one from home and one from Reggie. I am still in the firing line, this being the thirteenth day. I have not seen any of my battalion since the last time I told you of, but I heard Stan is quite well (that was yesterday) and that Bob Chessman had gone home with a wounded arm. I am pleased to hear that you are meeting some of your friends and enjoying little outings which will make the time pass more pleasantly and a little quicker.

You must thank Grace for me, for taking care of you as she seems to be doing.

There have been drastic changes in the Government, I hear. I hope it is for the best. The best news we have had is that Italy has joined in. What an awful affair the troop train smash was?

Well my, dear, there is nothing else to talk about, so please excuse more until the next green envelope.

I am still quite fit. With heaps of love, Yours, Ted

Footnotes to No. 27:

1 Italy declared war on Austria on 23 May 1915.

2 A troop train derailment near Gretna Green resulted in more than 200 deaths.

No. 28 29 May 1915

I have not received a letter from you since the one you wrote last Sunday but I know you have written and I know you wait for this from me. I am short of paper so please don't mind this half sheet. This is my fifteenth day in the firing line. I have had no news of Stan or Charlie for some days. The 20th. made a good charge last night, turning a German attack to a British attack and capturing some trenches. I hear that the casualties were not heavy but I am very anxious for more news. All this took place a little along the line so I was not in it. I am with the 17th. Battn. holding a position on the canal bank.

Now my dear, I must close with a loving au revoir.

Ever yours, Ted

P.S. I am still quite fit, getting quite brown.

No. 29 31 May 1915

I had a red letter post yesterday, two letters from you dated 18th and 25th, the former containing the returned one of the 2nd, two letters and a parcel from home and a parcel of chocolate from the office. Quite a collection! I am still in the firing line and have had no news of the battalion for some days. I hear that our Brigadier has been killed. We are expecting to be relieved for at least a short time, tomorrow I think, by the Canadians. I wish I were coming to Bournemouth with you. Oh! What a time we could have together. Give my kind regards to Grace. I think it quite a good idea for her to write to me and you to her soldier but you must still write to me as well. I am still quite fit and well despite the fact that I was nearly blown up yesterday by a shell.

I hope you are quite well and that you will have good weather and a decent holiday. The rest should do you worlds of good. The war may be over in time for me to have at least a summer week-end at the seaside and if so you shall be there too.

Now my dear, there is nothing more to write about so once more au revoir.

With heaps of love, Ever yours, Ted

Main Street, Maroc 1915. *Photo: Imperial War Museum*

JUNE 1915

At the beginning of June 1915 the French handed over to the British the front from the La Bassée canal south to the west of Lens and the 47th. Division spent the summer in one or other of the three sectors into which this segment of the Western Front was divided – 'Y' in front of Vermelles, 'X' opposite the village of Loos-en-Gohelle and 'W' from Loos to the French front facing Lens. The Divisional HQ was mostly at Verquin with the Divisional Artillery HQ in mine buildings at Les Brébis. The centenary day of the Battle of Waterloo, 18 June 1915 found the 47th. Division holding the right of the British line near Maroc, adjoining the French.

The 20th. London moved on 1 June marching to Sailly la Bourse before relieving the 1st. Cameron Highlanders the next night, in the trenches in front of Vermelles. This relief involved a difficult slow journey of an hour and a half along communication trenches passable only under cover of darkness. In its turn the Battalion was itself relieved four nights later by the 2nd. Coldstream Guards and by 4 a.m. on 7 June it reached billets in Verquin for twelve hours' rest before moving on again by night. For four days, Battalion HQ and 'A' and 'C' Companies were located in Mazingarbe and 'B' and 'D' Companies in Philosophe. The 20th. provided night working parties to repair the reserve trenches. One of these working parties attracted enemy attention one night and was badly shot up.

During a 24 hour spell holding a section of the sector 'X' front 1,500 yards west of Loos, the battalion was occupied mainly in trench repair, before returning to Mazingarbe. The threat of a German attack on 16 June caused the 20th. to be rushed to positions in trenches on the north-east side of the slag heaps of Fosse no. 6 at les Brébis but the attack did not materialise. The battalion was stood down and returned to Mazingarbe which came under enemy shell-fire on the 19th.

For the next eight days the 20th. were in a subsector of the 'W' front east of Grenay where the opposing front line trenches were some 350–500 yards apart. This was a "quiet" period devoted to consolidating trenches; Battalion HQ was located "in the middle of the slag heap" at Fosse no. 5 Maroc. The miners' cottages close behind the trenches were still occupied by the civil population; 'C' Company's trenches were flooded in a thunderstorm on 25 June.

Relieved by the London Irish Rifles (18th. London) on 28 June, the 20th. retired to their billets in Les Brébis before marching down to South Maroc the next day to take over another section of sector 'W' from the

17th. London. After four days they in turn were relieved by the "Shiny Seventh" (7th. London) and marched back to Philosophe.

No. 30 — 3 June 1915

My dear,

Thanks for your letter of the 30th ult. We have been relieved from the position we were in. We came out on the 1st and reached the town where we were to "rest" at about midnight and left again the next afternoon and came up here into the trenches again yesterday. I had time enough however to get a nice hot bath at a bathing establishment and a good feed. I and a corporal of the 18th. spent most of the morning in a pastry shop. How long we are in for this time, I cannot say but this seems to be a quieter part of the line.

I went along to that part of the line held by the 20th. this morning and saw Stan and Leo. Both are quite well. I could not find my company. They were back in the reserve trenches so I had no news of Charlie. Stan is now a full corporal and if I had been with my company I expect I should have had a promotion.

I hope you are having decent weather and that the change and rest are already doing you good.

The weather here is superb – just ideal for a summer holiday.

I am still quite fit and going on merrily.

Give my regards to Grace. Once more au revoir, my dear.

With all my love, ever yours, Ted

P.S. Shall be glad of the sox.

P.P.S. I was unable to post this yesterday so I am adding a little this morning. Your parcel has arrived and is I assure you appreciated to the full. The pudding is fine. I am also glad of the socks, the fruit and in fact everything is very welcome. Thank you very much. I am expecting a letter today sometime.

No. 31 — 15 June 1915

You must really forgive me for not writing before. This is the second day we have been back from the trenches. We were in for over a month except for two nights when we moved. At the first opportunity I should have written but I have been so busy. We all had lost something or other and we have been refitting etc. I have lost count of the actual period we were in for, so that just shows you the state I had got into. I did not even know the day of the week. We are out of the firing line but are still shelled a little. A fellow was killed by a shell and several wounded quite near here yesterday. We have had quite a job cleaning up and yesterday we got a bath – a cold tub and a hose pipe.

I have seen Stan, Charlie and Leo. They are all quite well.

Thank Grace very much for her letter and postcard. I will reply in your next green envelope, tomorrow. I am quite fit but the heat is very trying especially as I am wearing a new pair of boots. There is very little news despite the lapse in my correspondence but perhaps the green envelope will be more interesting.

I am so pleased you have had such a nice holiday. You certainly had topping weather. Once again, dear, a loving "au revoir".

Yours ever, Ted

No. 32 **18 June 1915**

I have received your letter of last Sunday. Thanks very much. We are still resting although we have several parades per day. I have also seen the paragraph re "Ivanhoe" in the "Mercury" you kindly sent, but I think they have made a mistake or two.

We had an alarm the night before last and were rushed up to the trenches for an attack or something.

You have had a fine time, I should think, at Bournemouth. I should not mind having a fortnight in flannels at some seaside place. I expect the office will be a bit dull after. But cheer up. I should not mind being at the office again. We are all looking forward to "après la guerre" and I can assure you I am, as I know you are. I just long to once more hold you in my arms. I could then tell you all about it and I will one day. There is such a little I can put in a leter, but I do want you Oh! so much. Do not worry dear, I love you so that I cannot see anything but happiness for us both when I return. I expect a letter in today's post. I just pine for your letters, they are so sweet to me.

I am still quite well and would not mind wagering that I am browner than you are, despite your sun baths.

Now dearest, I must close. Au revoir.

With heaps of love, Yours ever, Ted

No. 33 **20 June 1915**

I received your letter of the 15th and your parcel. It is so kind of you to send such a collection of nice things. The day before it arrived I received a similar one from my aunt at Forest Gate.

We are still resting. We had a Church Parade this morning in the grounds of a large building used as an RAMC hospital. The hospital staff band is out here and they played the hymns etc. It was quite like old times to march back with a band. They played selections, the other evening, in the town, much to the enjoyment of the inhabitants. There is really nothing in the way of news. We just have our parades and then amuse ourselves as best we can. We are having quite a decent time but I do not know how long it will last – not more than another day, I think.

I am quite well, but I have not seen Stan or Leo or Charlie.

This morning I went with a corporal of the 18th. to the early communion service. it is about the first Sunday that has been any different to the weekdays.

Now my dear, once more "au revoir".

With all my love, Yours ever

P.S. Kind regards to Mr. Randall and Miss Guymer. Please do not send jam or marmalade in any parcel out here. We get plenty of that. I appreciate your kindness absolutely to the full. Do not think this is ingratitude.

No. 34 **21 June 1915**

I received your little note of the 17th yesterday. We have made another move and are now in a town quite near the trenches waiting our turn to go up. I am in a most "comfy" billet. The people seem to be unable to do enough for us. It is quite a small house – a miner's cottage in fact. I saw Charlie last night when his platoon marched through on the way up to the line.

You must find my letters very uninteresting, but there is really such a little to write about and one cannot say anything about what we are really doing.

I am still quite well. how is my little girlie? Quite well too I hope. I do wish I could seen how you are for myself. It would be just lovely to just pop home for just a wee while, so that we could have just a little time all to ourselves. What a lot we could find to talk about then! But cheer up, dear, that day will one day come and we shall then be more to each other, through this period of separation. I just long for your sweet presence. The weather just makes one yearn for the river, tennis etc. and of course these thoughts are, with me, just full of you. I often pity the fellows out here who seem to have no girlie to write to and from whom to receive letters. Your letters mean so much to me. I read them again and again and wonder how many more times we must say au revoir.

Once more must I use this means of sending you my love. Au revoir.

Ever yours, Ted

P.S. Please give the enclosed love letter to Grace.

No. 35 **24 June 1915**

I have not received a letter from you recently but I know that is not your fault. Will you please, in future, underline "Trench Mortar Battery" heavily, on the address.

I am still in the comfortable billet I told you of, but the town is becoming less comfortable as the Huns have shelled it on two occasions. Just after writing your last letter I had a most remarkable escape. A shell dropped in the street about 15 yards from me and the fellow I was with was wounded in three places, two others behind me were wounded slightly and a poor little boy was wounded not five yards from me. I took him in a house and commenced to bandage him but despite the efforts of the Red Cross people who took him to hospital the poor little chap died this morning. Another boy was badly wounded and a civilian was killed. It is terrible to think that so many women and children run such a risk by living in the danger zone but they are so reluctant to leave their homes. There have also been several soldiers killed and a lot wounded here by the shells. This place had hitherto been immune from the barbarians.

There is little else to tell you except that I am quite well and altho' sorry to lose three comrades from the battery and see children hurt, still in good spirits.

Once again I assure you of my love and say a loving au revoir.

Yours, Ted

No. 36 — 27 June 1915

I received your letter of the 23rd this morning. I am still in this village and still quite well. Expect we shall go up in the line tomorrow.

The time seems to go quite quickly out here but I expect it hangs with you. I would have just loved to have been with you at Maidenhead. I can picture the scene well but surely there was a scarcity of men to make things go as they should? (Eh! What!)

Cliveden is an admirable place for a hospital, isn't it?

The musician at the Queens Hall was evidently a person with a strong sense of humour or else a lunatic or perhaps an excessive drinker.

Please go on going out with your girl friends.

Last Sunday was certainly a nice change but today is just like a week day on which the people don their "Sunday bests" (if any).

I was very sorry to hear of Lt. Warneford's death.

You know Charlie is not with me. He is a bomb thrower for hand grenades (the VC winners).

There is really no more news. I have written two little notes which I should be obliged if you would post for me. It saves the officers trouble in censoring. I still look forward with you to a future in each other's company. Au revoir, my beloved.

With all my love, Yours, Ted

P.S. I have another green envelope in hand.

P.P.S. Please put a few bachelor's buttons and another tin of lemonade powder in your next parcel.

Footnote to No. 36:
Flight Sub-Lieut. R. A. J. Warneford V.C., R.N. was one of the earliest air "aces" of the war.

No. 37 **30 June 1915**

I have received your letter and parcel of the 24th the latter arriving yesterday. I believe I failed to acknowledge receipt of the "Mercury" and "Punch" a few days ago. Thanks so much for them. I am up in reserve now just behind the line and yesterday I ran across some of my old section. One of them had a birthday the day before and heaps of good things in parcels so he had a tea party in a little shed. It was a jolly turn out. Stan was with me and there were seven others besides the host. Yesterday and today we have had a swim in the huge tank under the condenser in a local mine and the day before I had a fine hot bath and cold douch in the miners' bath house.

Your Dad's letter of the 12th has not yet reached me.

Elsie wrote on the 24th that she and Will were going to Bournemouth on the 25th. Are they staying there?

Did Grace get my letter? At least, what did she say about it?

There is nothing more in the way of news for you. You know how I just long for your presence and when that is impossible, your letters. So you see I think so often of you. I am always thinking of you. Au revoir my darling.

With much love, Yours ever, Ted

Dear ———
"At present we are staying at a farm . . ."

See Letter No. 156 From *Fragments from France* – Bruce Bairnsfather.

JULY 1915

On 10 July the 20th. was cheered by the granting of home leave to the Commanding Officer, Colonel E. J. Moore, Capt. Hooper, the RSM and the three men who had won the DCM at Givenchy. Inevitably hopes were raised of a regular leave rota being set in motion but sadly these were not to be realised. Platoons returned individually to Mazingarbe and preparations were made for an inspection of all the transport of 141 Brigade at Houchin on 12 July.

The following day Ted Trafford returned from the Trench Mortar Battery and rejoined 'B' Coy. in no. 8 platoon. The 20th. was back in the line again on 14 July when they relieved the 22nd. London. 'B' Coy. occupied keeps E, F, G and H north of the Lens – Béthune road with 'C' and 'D' Companies in support, billeted in Quality Street. 'A' Coy. was held in reserve at Fosse no. 7.

This was a period of heavy night work reconstructing the defences. There was heavy enemy shelling on 17 July especially near the Lens road and Sap 18, but 'B' Coy. remained in the keeps until relieved by the 8th London (Post Office Rifles) on the 30th.

No. 38 **3 July 1915**

My dear Pattie,

Thanks so much for your sweet little note of 28th. It is dear of you to promise to write *more* often. As it is I think you write me very frequently but I know I cannot get too many if I got two a day.

I had Leslie Barrett's letter this morning. Isn't he a jolly little youngster?

I think that the idea of a cucumber in your last parcel was a jolly good one. Salmon and cucumber for "brekka" was a pleasant change.

I saw Charlie a couple of days ago. He was looking quite fit and well.

I am now in the trenches and have seen Stan "up the line" this morning. I am afraid the French "parlez" is not getting on very well "avec moi" but by using very bad grammar and making statements (of not more than three words) with a note of enquiry in my voice I can ask questions. In this manner and with many gesticulations I can carry on a limited conversation with the French "soldiers, villagers, policemen and chorus".

We are in a fresh position and the trenches are in quite a picturesque part in cornfields with more poppies, cornflowers and wild flowers than corn. The weather is stinging hot and our dugout is swarming with flies. They are a great pest.

The French and German artillery continue an overhead duel day and night with our "heavies" occasionally joining in. We were watching the shells burst last night. It was quite a display.

Now, my dear, there is but one more item of news and that is that I am quite well, with that, and a loving "au revoir", I will close.

With all my love, Your Ted

P.S. I hear through Bert Giles that Reggie is engaged!!!

No. 39 — 5 July 1915

Since writing you last I have not had another letter from you. I know you have written but I do feel it a big blank when I know I have missed some of your letters. I came out of the trenches in the early hours of this morning and am back in my nice little billet. I hope you are quite well. I am and Stan was when I saw him last. He sends his kind regards to you and your Dad. As I also do. This must be a short letter as there is no news and I have not got one of your letters to reply to. I know nothing whatever about the leave you mention as rumoured, but do not be surprised if one day, during the next six months I come a-knocking at your door. I send you all my love and I know my dear that my feeling is reciprocated. I am lucky to have someone to love and by whom I am loved.

Au revoir, darling. Yours, Ted

No. 40 — 7 July 1915

Quite well! Will write fully tomorrow.

Ted

No. 41 — 8 July 1915

I have received your letter of the 3rd, but rumour has it that letters from England are now censored somewhere en route and are consequently delayed. I am still out of the trenches and today am not feeling quite up to scratch but I shall be quite ok by tomorrow. We were turned out at 5 a.m. this morning for a bath parade. We had plenty of hot water and tubs at a little brewery near here.

There is much subdued excitement here about leave but we know nothing about it in the battery yet.

Some men in the brigade (quite a few) have gone home for a week, today.

I do not know when my turn will come. I want it for one thing more than anything else and that is to be with you for a little while. Just to hold you close and tell you all about it. What a lot we should have to cram into those few days – if I am lucky enough to get any leave. Do not anticipate it too much or you may be disappointed. I do hope, though, that you will not be. I hope you are not being too overworked on account of the extra work owing to the War Loan.

Glad to hear of your investments. I shall put in a little when I get the opportunity. I think I will write to Dad about it now. Your Dad was very good to do as he did for you. Wasn't he? I am trying to send home a German hand grenade as a souvenir. I have taken all the explosive out so that it is quite safe. It dropped in the trench and gave us all a bit of a scare, but luckily for us it failed to explode.

Now my dear, once more I must close with "au revoir".

With all my love, Yours ever, Ted

P.S. Have not seen Charlie or Stan for some days. Kindest regards to your Dad and all your friends who know me.

No. 42 — 10 July 1915

I received your letters of the 6th yesterday and of the 4th the day before. I am feeling better today although for two days I have not been quite as well as usual. Stan also I am sorry to say has not been quite himself for a day or two. There is however every prospect of a move to a place where we shall at least be out of range for shells, a condition which has not existed now for over two months. I learnt that *the* battalion were in the next village so last night I strolled over to see Stan and my other pals. I found Stan's billet and had not been there for ten minutes when I heard a well known voice asking for Corporal Ted Trafford. We went out and who do you think confronted us? – Alec Anderson. He had arrived the previous night and joined his battalion in a ruined village, the next, on the further side from here, to Stan's. How lucky that I happened to be there. It was an exciting meeting. We walked down to his billet but of course could not stay long. He was going up to the trenches for the first time last night with a working party to do some digging. He looks remarkably fit and he said I did. I also saw Leo, who sends his kind regards. He doesn't seem as well as he might. I think we are getting "stale". Charlie looked quite well.

Please thank Grace for her promise to write soon. I hope she won't "tell off" her soldier too much in her next letter to him.

You wonder how we get water. Well all pumps etc. are first tried by the R.A.M.C. and a notice put up "For Washing" if fit. All drinking water is drawn from our water carts which are filters and carriers combined. Should we have to get our water from a source other than the cart, it must first be boiled or else a sterilising tablet used. We get a little supply of these occasionally. I have a good stock. You mention an occasion when D.S.O.s were won by officers. Four men of the 20th. got D.C.M.s on the same occasion, and incidentally those men have gone on leave. I am writing a letter or two for my pals at home and shall be greatly obliged if you will post them off for me. I am also going to write, with many references to the dictionary, to a sergeant in the French artillery with whom I became friendly. He is a lawyer and a jolly fine chap.

Well, darling, I suppose it does seem a long while since that eventful night at

St. Albans. The time flies by day with me, but when I look back, so much has happened that it seems a long time since I last saw your dear face with those eyes of yours – such eyes – just brimming. Dearest don't think I am saying this to upset you but that night always remains with me in memory along with many more pleasant remembrances.

How I hope it will not be too long before we again continue hand in hand the chain of pleasant memories.

Au revoir, my beloved. Yours, Ted

P.S. Kindest regards to your Dad and friends.

No. 43 **13 July 1915**

Thanks so very much for your parcel and letter of the 8th. I am now back to the battalion so in future please address your letters to me in no. 8 platoon, 'B' Company. I expect I shall miss some of your letters for a few days as they will need to be redirected from Brigade Headquarters.

Do not think that your letters ever bore me. They always have just the opposite effect. I am glad you find a little consolation in my letters. I only wish they could convey more.

I am resting for a few days at the Ambulance Station as I have been a bit out of sorts for nearly a week. You must not worry or think I am ill. I am just slightly indisposed and not at all in the mood for letter writing at present, so please excuse more today.

With all my love, Yours, Ted

P.S. Please thank Aunt for the cake.

No. 44 **16 July 1915**

I do hope you have not worried too much about me. I am not so very bad although for a day or two I have felt rather "cheap". The "rest at the ambulance station" soon came to an end and I was sent to a field hospital where I now am. The "ward" is a little marquee and the "bed" is a stretcher. The "nurses" are R.A.M.C. men who do their best for us. The hospital is in a delightful spot, truly rural and quite pretty.

My trouble is a form of Gastritis(?) caused no doubt through eating too much tinned food or through the swarms of flies. I expect to go on to light, instead of milk diet, tomorrow and to get up in a couple of days. I do not get letters. They are kept by the battalion for me. I have not heard from you since last Sunday.

I trust that you are quite well and that you will not worry your dear little self about me.

With all my love, Yours, Ted

No. 45 **18 July 1915**

Another Sunday has come round and I am pleased to say that I feel far more my old self than I did last Sunday. Had I got over this little illness in a day or two I should have said nothing about it so as to cause you no undue anxiety, but the fact that I have been unable to reply to your letters would have given the show away so I made a "confession" of the whole affair. I am a lot better now and hope to get up tomorrow. I have had real food today – the first change from a milk diet since last Monday. I wish I could get your letters. I do miss them so. More I think now than at any time, if it be possible to make a distinction. I shall have a nice lot when I get back. Quite a sheaf of them!

I hope you and your Dad are both well.

I wrote and thanked you for your last parcel but I have another "confession". I have not been able to touch any of the good things yet. The cake and tinned fruit I passed on to Stan, who I am sure appreciated their worth, while the remainder is in my pack waiting for "the day".

I hope to be out of here very soon if for no other reason than to get your letters.

Once again then, my dear, au revoir.

With all my love, Yours, Ted

P.S. Don't send another parcel until you hear I am out.

No. 46 **20 July 1915**

You will be pleased to hear that I am now well on the road to recovery. I have been allowed to get up today. Naturally, after being off my feet for a week I felt a trifle weak, but I went for a little stroll and I expect it is only a matter of a few days before I shall return to my battalion quite well again. I am still without letters and cannot help wondering whether all is well with you. I hope that you are quite well and that nothing has happened, of course other than this awful war, to mar your happiness.

I do hope, although something seems to tell me I hope in vain, that you have not worried over my little malady. I am sorry if you have, but at the same time it fills me with a happy thrill to know that you care enough to be worried over me. I do long for a line from you. Your letters are to me as a little of personality sent thro' the post to comfort and inspire me. Without them for any length of time life here would be almost unbearable. I am hoping to get some sent on from the battalion, as I have written them to let them know which field ambulance I am with. It will be a red letter day when they arrive.

Now, Pattie dear, I must again say "au revoir".

With all my love, Your Ted

Kindest regards to your Dad, your friends and Miss Guymer.

No.47 22 July 1915

I am going on well and hope to be discharged soon.

Letters follows at first opportunity.

I have received no letter from your lately.

Ted

No. 48 23 July 1915

I am still anxiously waiting for the post which will bring a letter for me. I am now fit again and hope to rejoin the battalion tomorrow. I have been out for a walk on several occasions. There are some beautiful woods hereabouts and when walking through them I could not help thinking how happy we two might have been there together. There is such a little to tell you about. I just do nothing all day but stroll about. It is nice to get a rest but I want to get back to the battalion. How I wish I could just get a letter from you.

Au revoir, my love, Yours, Ted

No. 49 26 July 1915

I am now back with the battalion and in the trenches with my old section again – it is good to be back with them. I saw Stan last night on my way up. He is quite well. I was discharged from hospital on Saturday, but had to travel in short stages with long intervals. I arrived with the supplies on A.S.C. waggons. I was very disappointed to find only two of your letters waiting for me – one written on the 10th and one on the 11th. Both old ones by now. What has happened to subsequent ones I have been unable to discover.

I am feeling quite fit again and I hope to hear from you very shortly that you are keeping quite well.

There is little more to say just at present so "au revoir" once more.

With all my love, Yours, Ted

No. 50 28 July 1915

I have at last got a fairly recent letter from you, the one you wrote on Friday last. I am looking forward to the Sunday one which should arrive today.

I had a very strenuous day yesterday – digging and building a dug-out, and filling and carrying sand bags to repair and make alterations in trenches.

We have made a very elaborate shell proof dug-out, right underground. The floor is boarded as is also the roof which is supported by heavy beams. The front is to be decorated with a white horse in chalk and we have a small flight of steps – "pinched" from a wrecked coal mine – in the entrance. We carried all the wood up from this mine. It is quite a triumph of art and engineering.

A Scottish regiment has been in the trenches with us for instruction and I think we shall be relieved soon for a good period of rest.

I hope you and all at home are quite well. I feel quite fit again, but I want you. Au revoir, my dear.

With all my love, Yours, Ted

P.S. Stan tells me there was a parcel for me while I was away. He opened it and to prevent it being wasted utilized the contents. I want the socks though and he is going to pass them on to me.

No. 51 **30 July 1915 2 a.m.**

I am on night watch and there is very little to do at this unearthly hour. I naturally began to think of home and you, which prompted me to write you a letter.

We are being relieved this evening so I shall not be able to post this today.

It is a glorious morning – just getting light and the sky is lovely. I did not get much sleep. We did not turn in until midnight and I have just been roused out again. We had a concert last night, which accounts for our late hours. Our Captain, Captain Escombe DSO, who, by the way is going on leave tomorrow to be decorated by the King, borrowed a gramaphone (sic) and brought it into our dug-out. We had such an awful crowd in the cramped space, all smoking, and the air was like a fog. The records were fine ones and the machine a splendid phoneless one. Fine! That is all just for the present.

31 July 1915

We are now out of the line and back a little way.

We are billeted in a huge barn with straw to sleep on. We have had a very busy day, cleaning our equipment and clothing. It poured with rain yesterday afternoon just before our relief arrived. A terrific thunderstorm with tons of rain soon caused the trenches to become miniature canals. The trenches in this part were dug in chalk so you can imagine what we looked like – white from head to feet. We waded out with water nearly to our knees, the while under an indifferent shrapnel fire which luckily caused no casualties. We got into our billet soon after dark and slept well. Our boots and socks are still wet today.

Dad has taken 2 – £5 shares out for me. I shan't take any more because as you say we shall want money ready to hand one day.

The souvenir I was sending came back to me. The authorities have stopped us sending things like that thro' the post. This letter will not be posted today as I had not time to finish it before post (mid-day).

Sunday morning 1 August 1915

It is a grand morning and we have been out doing ordinary drill this morning and have some more to do this afternoon.

I sent my grenade home by a pal going on leave. If it gets through all right, I will write you his address when he comes back and you can then fetch it.

How do you like a serial letter?

Stan and I went out to "brekka" this morning and we got some fine champagne in an estaminet near here last night. It is quite cheap out here – for champagne. Now my dear, the censor will wonder when I am going to shut up, so it must again be au revoir.

With all my love dearest, Yours ever, Ted

P.S. Leo is quite well and sends kind regards.

P.P.S. So sorry to hear your Dad has been so queer. I hope he is better now. I am still fit.

1393 L/Cpl. Ted Trafford and 1539 Pte. Leo Shurly, Hatfield, 1914.

AUGUST 1915

The 20th. was congratulated by the Divisional Commander on its trench reconstruction and was withdrawn from the forward area on 3 August. It was a difficult night march in wet dark conditions from Mazingarbe via Noeux-les-Mines and Haillicourt which brought the battalion to Allouagne by 07.30 hours on the anniversary of the outbreak of war.

Since arrival in France the 20th. had sustained relatively light battle casualties – one officer killed and two wounded, with other ranks 29 killed and died of wounds, 6 missing and 150 wounded. Sickness casualties amounted to 5 officers and 378 other ranks, of whom about 253 returned to duty.

141 Brigade was now in Corps reserve for nearly a month of recreation and re-training and the assimilation of replacements.

Activities recorded in the Battalion War Diary for this period included a sing-song in the chateau courtyard at Allouagne on 7 August; a Battalion sports meeting on the 14th; a Brigade Church Parade on the 15th (spoilt by rain squalls); and route marches (via Lillers, Ecquedec and Hurionville) on the 16th and through Lapugnoy to Houchin on 18 August traversing the Bois des Dames where mud caused great problems for the transport column.

The second half of August was devoted to repairing and digging new trenches and in intensive training for a supposed new offensive. After four days digging a new third line trench east of Noeux-les-Mines, there was a break for bathing at Barlin followed by a Divisional Sports Meeting near Allouagne and then on Saturday 28 August a Church Parade with the 19th. London and the 5th. London Field Ambulance in a field west of Houchin where the preacher was the Bishop of Khartoum. Two days later the 20th. moved back by motor bus to Les Brébis to occupy billets vacated by the 17th. London. There was an immediate resumption of night work; the first task was to dig new communication trenches from the second line to sector W3 and to the right of X1; the second to prepare a new front line in front of W2 and south of the Béthune – Lens road. The battalion was pulled back again in the early hours and transported by motor bus from Les Brébis to Houchin where it arrived at 04.30 hours on 2 September in rain, to bivouac in fields to the west of the village. The rain persisted for thirty-six hours while the men rested under miserable conditions.

No. 52 **3 August 1915**

Dearest,

I have received your letters of 13th, 15th, 17th and 18th July enclosed in yours of the 29th and 31st and am so sorry to hear that you were feeling so "down". Do cheer up my dear. I know it is harder for you than me. You have no jolly comrades to keep your spirits up and no excitement to keep your mind occupied, but know this that I always think of you and wish I could make you happy.

The enclosed was taken at Festubert, behind the line, some three months ago. It is an enlargement of a very tiny photograph taken with a vest pocket camera. The original, I am told, was clearer although so small. I am trying to get a copy. We are sitting around a brazier cooking our breakfast. The roof as you will see is quite whole, about the only one in the village, although the front of the house had suffered a little. Three of the fellows in the group have been wounded since, while another has had his nerves shattered. "Dolly" Dray, who by the by, lives in George Lane, and whose face can just be seen behind mine, is in England, home I believe, with his face badly damaged by a bomb. Alec Wilson who is bending down so that only his hat and ear can be seen is home with a wounded arm. The other wounded chap is back with us and the fellow whose nerves suffered is standing up on something at the back. In case you don't recognise me with my hair almost shaven, I am the central figure on the old chair. Stan says he is sorry he forgot to acknowledge the parcel intended for me but he was in the trenches at the time. His opinion of your cake is that it was a "topper". As good as any he has had, so I am looking forward to the next.

I have got the socks now. So don't be cross with him any more. Charlie seems quiet well. I cannot understand why he should have got someone else to write for him. Leo thanks you for your kind regards and sends his. I have not seen any more of Alec nor have I run across the 71st. Brigade Royal Field Artillery.

I should have liked to see you and Grace doing that cooking. I know it was funny. By the way you might thank her for her letter. I wonder you censored it and let it pass.

Of course, just now we are all thinking of what we were doing twelve months ago and I naturally remember how you came to see us off to camp on the Sunday morning and our return so suddenly and all that has happened since to make you unhappy. Oh how I wish it were in my power to make you quite happy now at once.

I am quite well and I hope by now that you are. You did not say in your last letter.

Bob Hapgood is still in my section and has been in hospital but is better now.

I hope your Dad is better now. Give him and Miss Guymer my kindest regards. Yesterday being bank holiday and we being in a fair sized town, we – that is I and three other fellows – went out to lunch at a show where we had pork cutlets, chipped potatoes and champagne. In the evening evening Leo and I walked over to a mine in a village near here and had a glorious hot bath – a greater luxury than the feed.

Now my dear, I suppose I shall have to ease up or I shall be late for guard. A job I have got for tonight. I will just try to cheer you up a bit by assuring you that my love for you is as strong as ever. I just long for you. How I would like to fold you in my arms and tell you how I love you. It would be delightful to kiss away the tears I know would come through absolute joy. I will one day and you shall be happy.

Au revoir, my love, Yours, Ted

No. 53 **5 August 1915**

A year ago today! What a lot has happened since then, but just for the present it is hard for me to realize that we are taking part in anything much worse than annual training. We are now at the town where we stayed about four months ago, before we went up to the line at all. I went on guard on Tuesday evening at six o'clock at the town we were then in. We moved off with the battalion at 11pm and marched until 2am when we had an hour's rest and some hot tea. We marched again from three to six. As soon as we arrived here I continued the guard until 7.30 last evening, so I did not get a sleep for about 40 hours. When I did, I DID!

Tell Grace I will write in reply to her note in your next green envelope.

This place is almost unrecognisable now. It seemed, in last March, to be such a dreary place but now in its summer garb it is quite pretty.

We have had a drill this morning and are having some more this afternoon. Our billet is a barn with straw for beds, next to an an estaminet, where we can get a feed. We are having a supper party tonight. The "we" is my section. The chief item of menu is to be rabbit. Quite a change!

You mentioned in your letter about young Squire's souvenir pipe. Strange to say, when we were in the trenches at Givenchy for a long stretch some six weeks ago, I started one. I got as far as the rampant horse on the front and cut one name on it. I shall finish it one day. Your parcel has just arrived. Thanks so much, it all looks so nice. I will give an opinion on the cake tomorrow.

Thanks for your letter of Sunday.

With all my love, Yours, Ted

No. 54 **8 August 1915**

I have just received your letter of the 4th. I got yours of the 2nd two evenings ago. You seemed so unhappy when you wrote that. You must not think that your friends did not want you because they did not ask you to go anywhere. Perhaps they thought the same because you did not suggest something for them to do with you, and you must certainly not think that no-one cares what you do. There is a fairly substantial "no-one" on this side of the "silver streak" who is just a wee bit interested; but I mustn't scold you. I know and understand exactly how you feel.

Your early attempts at cakemaking were certainly a great success. The sample I had was just as a cake should be, and shall be pleased to place an order for the rest of your stock at the price quoted. Several others had a taste and I told them all that you had made it. We cut it quite ceremoniously and they all said I was certain to be able to eat your cakes if nothing else so I should not starve in my old age. Everything else in the parcel was excellent as its quick disappearance amply testified.

Our rabbit supper was quite a success the evening before last and not so very expensive either. We are still "resting" with plenty of drill to keep us up to scratch and prevent slackness.

We are to have an al fresco battalion concert tonight. The weather is keeping fine and some of us are thinking of sleeping out, if we can secure a tarpaulin to rig up a shelter, in order to escape the rats who now disturb our sleep.

It seems so strange to write with a pen again. I have borrowed it from the people in whose barn we live. They are awfully good and have practically placed a room with table and chairs at our disposal.

I find I am always having to borrow a watch, when on guard and other duties. Would you mind sending mine out again with a new protector. The one I sent back on it had a broken spring. I should also like some tooth powder and a decent pencil. I have seen an advert for Freemans' Glass Oatmeal Lemon. It is like that lemon powder you often send out. I should very much like some, I think.

I saw Charlie this morning, he is quite well and we get on quite well together. Did you think we did not? He has a number of fellows in his own section with whom he usually goes out. I should think that the Service at St. Paul's was very impressive.

I am afraid you are not getting your proper amount of rest. You are missing your beauty sleep you know and must not do it.

There is not much more to write about now so I must soon close. I should just like to pop in to tea with you this afternoon; it would be fine. Au revoir, my love. I just want you so. I want you to creep close to me in my arms while I whisper how I love you.

Yours, Ted

Footnote to No. 54:
On 4 August 1915 the King and Queen attended a Drumhead Service of Intercession for the nation at St. Paul's Cathedral.

No. 55 **9 August 1915**

Thanks for your letter of the 6th. You seem a little more cheerful, in fact your letter was quite lively. I am glad you like the photo. You might thank the girl who paid me the compliment of likening me to Jack Johnson. Had the front of the house been shewn in the picture the real Jack Johnson "smile" would have been visible in a "yawning" hole. The grenade is now at Forest Hill and I will send the address if you would care to fetch it. The last letter I wrote was wrongly dated; it was written on the 7th not 8th.

Yesterday we had an open air Church service and had no other parades all day. In the afternoon Stan and I and another chap went into . . . . . [probably Lillers – Ed.], quite a large town near here. We had to have a pass and go in light marching order, with rifle and as it was quite a good distance and a hot day that rather took off the guilt. It was not a very interesting place, but we got our hair cut in a proper hairdressers' and heard English again spoken by two girls in a shop. They spoke English perfectly and how it reminded us of home and me of a little girl who I am just longing to hear talk to me.

The concert last night was a great success. The turns were all good and at the end we had a sketch entitled "Potted Potsdam". A fellow who is a "great" comedian impersonated Little Willie; the auther, an actor in private life, took the part of Wilhelm, perfectly, while Leo played "Von Hindenburg".

Today we have all had a glorious bath, but it was such a long march over the hills to the mine and the day was the hottest I have ever known – not sunny, but so sultry.

This evening we have had a miniature Hyde park Sunday evening. The 6th. R.A.M.C. band came over to play to us. It was fine but would have been finer if we had all had a fair companion to complete the Park illusion.

I am now laying on my straw bed and writing by candle light, and everyone is making such a row. But although they perhaps spoil my letter they do not interfere with my thoughts of you. You know I love you and I wait for the day when all this is over and we shall be together. Leave is granted to very small percentages each week. I may be lucky one day. I want to see you so much; but it's no use telling the Colonel that.

Now my dear I am just going to imagine I am kissing you good-night. Good night my beloved.

With all my love. Yours, Ted

P.S. Talking of the photo! No wonder I smiled. It was a cold morning and the breakfast was nearly ready.

No. 56 **12 August 1915**

Thanks so much for your letter of the 8th I received it last night. We are at the place where we had such cold weather when I was in the loft. The weather makes such a difference.

Yesterday we had quite a nice march. It was very hot though and today we have had a little rifle practice on such a dear little range in a sand quarry right in the middle of a pretty wood. We are having some company sports this evening as a preliminary to battalion sports on Saturday. I am still quite well. I saw Stan and Charlie this morning and they are both well. Charlie and I get on quite well together although I do not very often go out with him. There is really very little to write about. I am afraid this will be a very uninteresting letter as I do not feel in a mood for writing today. Of course that does not mean that I do not want to write to you. I think of you always.

This little souvenir came out of the wood we were in today.

I would just like you to be able to come down to see me as you used to at Hatfield. The chance of leave seems so remote and I want you so. Au revoir.

With all my love, Ted

No. 57 **Sunday 15 August 1915**

I have received your letter of the 10th this morning. It is a very fitful day today and the Church service (open air) was interrupted by frequent heavy showers. It seems fine just at present but how long it will last is still an open problem. Yesterday was quite fine and the battalion sports were quite a success. All events were run in service trousers and boots. That means a lot of races etc. It adds to the effort materially, but our company won many events. I was in our tug of war team and we reached the final which comes off tomorrow. We are a heavy and strong lot and should win. I also entered for the high jump and tied with two other fellows for the highest jump. We tried time after time to beat each previous effort but they decided in the end to call it a dead heat. That means that we shall all three jump in the brigade sports next Tuesday. The first three in each event representing the battalion in that event.

We have had a good dinner today off duck and green peas. It sounds rather extravagant and it is, but we do not often get the chance to indulge. I am afraid I have spent a lot of money lately. I have not had any sent out though, like some do. I have had very little army grub lately except breakfast when there is time for nothing else. It is a fine change.

I am glad things are smoother for you at home at present. I feel so sorry when I know you are not happy at home and I am powerless to improve matters. Poor little girlie I do sympathise with you. I understand just how you are placed, but whenever things go wrong try, my dear, to think of a rather big, lumbering, red faced chap our here who feels and cares for you.

Thanks for your letter which you had returned. I knew you were still writing in the same loving strain although I was not getting them at the time, and thanks also for the watch which reached me quite safely. I like wearing it again. It reminds, if any reminding is necessary, of you.

Thanks for remembrances to Charlie and Stan; they are both quite well and send kind regards. I am as fit as ever I was.

I suppose it it must be au revoir again, my dear.

With all my love. Ever yours, Ted

P.S. Just received your letter of the 12th. It is an awful shame to crush your hopes but really my dear the chances of leave are not at all great when one remembers that only four men per battn. go each week. They are just nominated but I think it is done in order of seniority. Glad you are going to spend the weekend with Elsie and Will.

P.S.S. The fellow's name who took the grenade home is Dangerfield and his home is at 7 Montem Rd Forest Hill.

Footnote to No. 57:
"Delts" Dangerfield, scrum-half for the Old Dustonians, was killed at Loos on 26 September 1915.

No. 58 — 17 August 1915

This is in further reply to your letter of the 12th which I acknowledged on Sunday. Yesterday we had a brigade route march. I marched just behind Charlie. It was quite a pleasant march although a bit hot.

In the evening we were victorious in the final tugs of war and five of our team including myself are in the eight to pull for the battalion this afternoon. Competitors were excused parades today so I am taking the opportunity to write. It has turned out a bit wet and it looks as if we shall be unlucky this afternoon as regards weather.

Last night we had a little farewell supper in our little "mess". One of our party, a sergeant major, is leaving to take up a commission so it was an occasion for much merriment although he is sorry to go and we are sorry to lose him. We broached more champagne but I think the opportunity for such luxuries will soon pass as we expect to leave here soon.

I sent home a French bayonet today, by a fellow, Spencer who you will remember at Hatfield, whose time has expired, but whether he will get it through is somewhat doubtful. It is a souvenir of our stay in the trenches at Vermelles some time ago and I took it from the equipment of a dead Frenchman. Only his equipment was left then. He had been buried.

I hope you had a nice time at Elsie's. I shall get your Sunday letter today I hope.

Well, dearest, I must begin to close with the sweet "nothings" which mean so much and which you know so well, but I do want you really. Au revoir beloved.

Yours, Ted

No. 59 **19 August 1915**

I received your letter of Sunday's date yesterday and your parcel this morning. I should have got that with the letter but we were moving and the parcels were kept until we reached our new destination. Thanks for the cake. I have not yet sampled it. Thanks also for the cigarettes, lemonade, bananas and toothpaste. The fruit was a bit squashed but quite eatable and when next sending tooth stuff please send a tin of powder as the paste is so liable to get squashed in the pack and it makes such a mess over other things if that happens. The brigade sports went off quite well on Tuesday afternoon. It was quite a pleasant affair. We had a band from the RAMC and much amusement was caused by a fancy dress competition. The fellows – about a dozen in all – were most weirdly attired in costumes they had made, begged, borrowed or stolen. Most of them were dressed as girls, one as a nigger, another as a broken down bookmaker, another as "the oldest inhabitant" while yet another appeared as a little boy in knickers and overalls and short socks.

On total points I regret to say the 18th. beat us but we were a good second and had we had some of our best athletes who are now home with wounds, we might have topped the list.

We won the tug-of-war in fine style and in the high jump I got third place. A "twentieth" man got first with five feet and I and an "eighteenth" man were able to clear only 4′ 11″. After failing three times at 5′ we had another three goes and he cleared at his last attempt. I was too heavy I think. Our battln. were leading by 5 points before the last event, the final of the quarter mile, but in that the "Irish" got 1st, 2nd and 3rd, with our men next. That put them up 35 points, but it was a jolly good afternoon and their wins were all jolly good ones.

In the evening we had a Brigade concert where we got our own back by supplying the chief "turn". "Potted Potsdam" appeared again and other items I described after our last battalion concert. Yesterday we made a move to a mean little village still well behind the line but not nearly so nice as our last place. From here we daily supply working parties who go up in shifts to dig trenches. My present billet is a kind of little mission hall with a fine concrete floor for sleeping on. Charlie is here as well, but he has part of the little wooden platform for his couch. We marched more or less across country, through some beautiful woods but owing to local thunderstorms the cart tracks were very muddy and made the going heavy. In places the transport waggons were only drawn by means of tow ropes on which we all hauled to help the horses.

I was detailed for headquarters guard today so I have not gone up with the diggers, although it means I shall not get much sleep tonight. The guard is from 7am to 7am. We of course were all sorry to leave our old billet but perhaps it's as well or we should have got too extravagant.

The "Guard Room" is a shed with only a roof and no walls in a yard. Not very comfy – Eh?

I am sorry I gave you the impression of being "down" in my letter of last Thursday. I was not as far as I knew, feeling very melancholy. Our platoon sergeant has left us to take a commission. He and the sergeant major I told you about went yesterday together, amid much cheering and "good-byeing!" That leaves this platoon with only one sergeant so don't be surprised if one day soon you have to slightly alter the mode of address of my letters.

I knew Grace was writing to a "Jock" and wondered if she would connect my anecdotes with the fact.

I came across some chaps in Guy Bush's battery (was it the 71st. or 171st.?) a week or two ago but they said they did not know him. Sorry to hear Wendon is ill. I hope it is not serious.

I am quite fit. So is Charlie and Leo and Stan. They both send kind regards. I trust your Dad is quite well and of course you know well that I hope you are. Keep as cheerful as you can, my dear. It will not be so very long.

Au revoir, my beloved. Yours, Ted

No. 60 — 21 August 1915

Thanks for your letter of the 17th. Since last writing you I have sampled the cake, in fact <u>we</u> have and the verdict is "good!!!" It's a jolly fine result for only the third attempt. We went on the early relief this morning and had finished our digging and returned to billets by 2pm. The mission hall I told you about which was intended for our billet is far too swarmed with flies to be comfortable or healthy so I, with a few others, have erected a bivouac tent with our ground sheets and some sacks in a field and sleep well in the open air. If the weather were very bad we still have our fly-infested building to tumble into.

There is nothing of interest in this village at all.

Did you see yesterday's "Daily Sketch"? It contains photographs of Captn. Thorne of this battalion and his wife, taken at their wedding, he being then on leave.

The loss of that transport ship was a grave affair and is another item on the bill which "Bill" must foot one day soon. I say soon advisably. You will hear of something happening in the near future. You must not drift into the ranks of the <u>All Is Lost</u> league.

Charlie is quite well, so is Leo and Stan. They both send kindest regards.

The watch is still going quite well.

That is all for the present, so once more, au revoir.

With all my love, Yours, Ted

Footnote to No. 60:
1000 men were reported missing when the British Transport Ship "Royal Edward" was sunk by a submarine in the Aegean Sea.

No. 61 **24 August 1915**

Thanks so much for your letters of 19th and 21st. I am still quite well and the battalion is having quite a busy time digging.

There is such a little to write about that I am afraid this will be quite short and uninteresting.

I shall be off parade tomorrow morning as the Brigade [Divisional – Ed.] sports are in the afternoon and I will then write far more fully.

With all my love. Yours, Ted

No. 62 **25 August 1915**

As promised, I am writing you this morning. The enclosed cards may interest you. I have not seen any of the places shewn thereon but the pictures are typical of the country.

Today is the day for our Divisional sports. We started with battalions when each company sent in representatives. The winners represented the battalion in brigade sports and the winners will today represent the brigades in the divisional contest. The competitors are going back in a motor lorry to the place where the affair is taking place, the rest of the battalion being still engaged in digging. I had a good rest this morning – not getting up until eight o'clock – although the company were on early turn and had to rise at five. It is a lovely morning and I feel as fit as the proverbial fiddle.

We should have a good time this afternoon. The programme is a long one and includes jumping and driving competitions for mounted officers and transport drivers.

The news of Russia's naval victory is reassuring and was received here with much enthusiasm. It was received by the signallers over the wire and published with battalion orders. We get daily papers – when we are in a more or less normal village – on the day following their publication, so by now we have details. The air raid at Walthamstow seems to have been very serious.

You seem surprised to hear that Spencer is coming home, but anyone whose four years have expired can, unless they sign on for an extra period, get home for good after serving an additional twelve months. His four years were up soon after we mobilized last year.

Glad to hear that you and Elsie had a little trip together on Friday.

There is really no more to tell you except what you know already and of which I know you will never tire, however often I repeat it. I love you and want you so.

Footnotes to No. 62:

1. In naval battles in the Gulf of Riga between 16 and 21 August, the Russians sank 2 German cruisers and 8 torpedo boats.
2. A Zeppelin raid on the Eastern counties of England on 17 August resulted in 10 civilian deaths and 36 injured.

At the present rate I think my leave should be due by the latter half of October, so don't wake up too early on Sunday mornings before then to see if I am outside. It is on Sunday mornings at about 5 am that leave men arrive home. Have you got my grenade yet? We shall have to lend it to Dad and Mother for a little while so that they may exhibit it among their friends, but it is ours – yours and mine – as I hope everything will be one day.

Once more, au revoir beloved. Yours, Ted

P.S. Did I acknowledge receipt of the Kentish Mercury? I believe I did not. Sorry. Thanks!

No. 63 — Saturday night 28 August 1915

Thanks for your letters of the 22nd and 24th the latter has arrived this evening.

The divisional sports were a great success as far as spectacular effect goes, but our brigade did nothing wonderful. We had no actual "dismal failures", yet nothing brilliant. We lost the tug to the team who were, eventually, champions. We were unlucky as, owing to military duties, we had to change three men for three strangers at the last moment. We had a selection of officers – crowds – ranging in rank from "boy" subalterns to General Sir Douglas Haig and including brigadiers, General of the Division and French officers of distinctive rank. There were some English Red Cross nurses and some French ladies. The ground, somewhat rough for a sports ground, was well decked with flags and looked quite refreshing in its natural setting in the midst of woods. We drove there and back, crowded in a motor lorry. Until today the digging continued in very hot weather, but today for a change we did battalion drill and were afterwards warned for a Church Parade this evening. It looks as if we are having it tonight instead of tomorrow. We have just come off this parade and it has started to rain. Bivouacks are not palaces when it rains. The service was a very impressive one. The ground on which it was held is on the top of a hill. Try and imagine it. The whole brigade formed up in close formation, like a square. In the centre is the band and a cart which is to serve as a pulpit, in which stand our Chaplain and the Bishop of Khartoum who has come to address us. Behind us is a valley and beyond that a plain of agricultural land, dotted with corn stacks, the whole bathed in the bluish evening mist. The sky is stormy and the sun is sinking in a blaze of red. Before us another plain already darkening with early night. Right away on the sky-line can be seen the occasional flash of bursting shells and the rumble and boom of distant cannonade is heard the while. The Bishop is a big man with a comforting presence and a big voice, and in the evening stillness every word rings. I can, without hesitation, say it was the most impressive service I have attended. It would have made a great picture. We were all in fighting order and carrying rifles.

That is about all I have to tell you, except that I haven't got room to write in our little tent. I hope it won't rain all night.

Now my dear, I hope you are keeping quite well; I am and Stan and Charlie and Leo all look as fit as fit.

I am glad to hear that you had Edith and sister to tea. You need company.

We shall not discard things like the Australians did or we shall be cold at nights. It's none too hot at 2am now.

You ask for an opinion about the holidays. Well, if people need a holiday and can get one, they should take one and I cannot see that it is selfish. If I were at home and could not join the army I should fail to see how I might help in the war any more at home than at the seaside. Again the war is a strain on most people's nerves and it is only right to recuperate.

Now, I think, I will tell you once more how I want you and how I long for the time when I can have you and you can have me, and we can just live in each other's love.

Good night, my beloved. Yours, Ted.

No. 64 **31 August 1915**

Thanks so much for your letter of 26th and your parcel. We made a move last night and are now in the town where I told you of that little fellow getting killed. It has suffered a terrible lot since I was here before. The house I had been billeted in is now a complete ruin. People still live here. We are going up this evening, as we did last, to dig advanced trenches. I have not much time so excuse rush.

I am quite well. I had to bring the parcel along unopened so I shall have to delay praise for your cooking until I have sampled it.

You must really excuse me now.

Au revoir, dear. With all my love. Yours, Ted

A street in Loos, September 1915.

Photo: Imperial War Museum

SEPTEMBER 1915 – LOOS

The 20th. was to be spared further front line duties until the big attack planned for the Loos front on 25 September, but this three week respite was fully occupied in the construction of new trenches and the carrying forward of supplies as well as simulation exercises for the forthcoming attack. The hub of these activities was Les Brébis where the tall spire of the Church in the village square made this a well-known target for the German artillery.

A joint Church Parade was held with the 19th. London on Sunday 5 September after which in the evening, 'A', 'B' and 'C' Coys. under Major Ball marched to billets in Les Brébis for daytime work on new trenches at North Maroc. On the 8th they returned to Noeux-les-Mines after dark for a full-scale Battalion exercise the following day in fields west of Houchin, for the forthcoming attack. The following evening saw the return of the 20th. by motor bus to Les Brébis, where packs were deposited before proceeding to North Maroc to work on a new support trench with communicating saps in W3 sector. The next night 'A', 'C' and 'D' Coys. toiled to produce a new trench in front of the crassier in W2, while 'B' Coy. was carrying supplies to the front line.

The 13 September found the Battalion billeted in Noeux-les-Mines in readiness for a combined rehearsal of assembly and attack with the 18th. (London Irish) and 19th. (St. Pancras) Battalions, on the same ground used for practice on the 9th September. After more trench digging the battalion reassembled in billets in Noeux-les-Mines during the evening of 15 September for a much enjoyed twenty-four hours rest, before another motor bus journey back to Les Brébis. Travelling in twenty-five buses at 100 yard intervals, the convoy was much delayed by horse transport and general traffic congestion as British troops packed into Noeux-les-Mines, Mazingarbe and Les Brébis. As a result only a short night's work strengthening the trenches in sector W3 was possible, after which the return to Les Brébis took three hours because of the congestion in the communication trenches.

Gas cylinders started to arrive on 18 September and the 15th. London (Civil Service Rifles) spent two hard nights carrying them to the specially prepared bays in the front line. Meanwhile, the 20th. had engaged in a final attack practice in the area between Noeux-les-Mines and Ruitz, and a four day artillery bombardment of the enemy positions had commenced. A violent thunderstorm on 23 September flooded the trenches to a depth of one foot but failed to delay the attack scheduled for dawn on Saturday 25 September.

The 20th. reached Maroc late on the Friday night; they had a hot meal and were joined by a section of a Field Company RE and two trench mortars; they entered the trench system at 01.30 hours 25 September and by 03.30 were in their assembly positions. 141 Brigade were on the left of the 47th. Divisional front (sector W3), joining the right flank of the 15th. Division; 140 Brigade in the centre (W2) and 142 Brigade on the right (W1) adjoining the French front.

Chlorine gas and smoke were released along the British front from 05.50 hours but there was insufficient wind to carry it eastwards to the opposing German line and it tended to accumulate in no-man's land and to drift northwards into W3.

The London troops attacked wearing their grey flannel respirators which after the first few hundred yards they rolled up on to the tops of their heads; the strange appearance of this headgear combined with faces blackened by smoke led some of the Germans to believe they were being attacked by Indians.

The London attack was to pivot on its right flank where in sector W1 the 21st. and 22nd. Battalions operated dummy figures as a diversion. In W3 the first wave of the 18th. (London Irish) left their trenches at 06.30 hours kicking a football ahead of them. The 19th. (on the left) and the 20th. (on the right) followed, passing through the Irishmen. The 20th. had gone over the top in four waves at one minute intervals from 06.35, their objectives being points south of the village of Loos – the "garden city", the copse and chalk-pit and the crassier (slag-heap). Tower Bridge was the name given by British troops to the twin pit-head gear immediately south of the village which gave enemy observers a commanding view over sector W of the battlefield; repeated efforts to demolish it by artillery fire had proved unsuccessful.

The Garden City was occupied by 07.00 hours and 'A' Coy. under Captain Guy Williams had captured the chalk-pit, where two field guns were concealed, by 07.30. The breech blocks of the guns were dropped down a well to ensure that the guns could not be brought back into use. These guns, with other trophies of war, were displayed on Horse Guards Parade in London later in 1915 and subsequently stood beside the entrance to the Battalion Headquarters at Holly Hedge House, Blackheath until disposed of to help the war effort during World War Two.

Meanwhile, 140 Brigade on the right of the 20th. had secured their objectives by 08.30, taking 300 prisoners and three machine guns in the process.

It proved impossible for the survivors of 'A' Coy. to capture the copse (a narrow spinney running south-west from the chalk-pit). Here the defenders held out for 48 hours "owing to the scarcity of grenadiers through casualties" (quotation from the Battalion War Diary). Consolidation of the ground gained was proceeded with and houses in the Garden City put in a state of defence as their cellars were cleared of startled French civilians and German army stragglers. The captured positions were maintained throughout the day only by constant effort and the left flank was left dangerously exposed where the 15th. Division had been forced to retire leaving a gap of nearly a mile to the 1st. Division opposite Hulluch. This situation was partially remedied on Sunday 26 September when the 23rd. London moved up to the Loos-Vermelles road and General Thwaites moved his Brigade HQ from Maroc to Valley Cross Roads on the outskirts of Loos. At the same time the 20th. was reinforced by units from the 17th. and 19th. Battalions, while Major W. H. Matthews was transferred out to take command of the 19th.

It had been a week-end of high achievement for the 20th. but also one of heavy losses; five officers were killed in action (Lieutenants Adams, Japp, Long, Thomasset and Young) and more than fifty other ranks. Two officers, Captain Hooper and Lieutenant Hamilton died of wounds within a few days; Major Ball, Captain Escombe DSO and Lieutenant Partridge were wounded and Captain Bell gassed.

On Monday 27 September the order came to attack the copse with a composite force under Colonel E. J. Moore CB VD, the Officer Commanding the 20th. London. A party from the 17th. (Poplar and Stepney Rifles) under Captain Wheatley with the grenadiers of the 17th. and 19th. Battalions, were to operate from the south-west corner, while the main attack from the north-east corner was to be made by a Company of the 23rd. London under Captain Ruthven with the grenadiers of the 20th. and 23rd. 'A' Coy. of the 20th. at the chalk-pit was to maintain covering fire with machine gun and rifle towards the south and frontal fire from the Y communication trench along the north-west side of the copse. The attack to be preceded by three hours of intense artillery bombardment and to coincide with an attack on Hill 70 by the Guards Division – led by the Scots Guards who advanced in open order through kale fields east of the village of Loos.

The infantry operation commenced at 16.50 hours and was entirely successful, the copse being captured by 19.30 and few casualties were suffered. But the toll of the defenders taken by the artillery barrage was tremendous and only three German prisoners were taken. The captured position was consolidated during the night by digging new trenches and a new front line was established and held throughout Tuesday.

The 24th. London (The Queens) from Kennington, relieved the 20th. at about midnight and it was a very tired depleted battalion that marched back into North Maroc at 02.30 hours on the 29th. for a day's rest before moving on to Quality Street that evening. A further move the following day brought them out of the fighting zone to fresh billets in Hesdigneul where on 1 October the Brigade Commander inspected and congratulated 141 Brigade.

No. 65 **3 September 1915**

Dearest,

Thanks so much for your two letters of the 29th and 30th. Glad to hear you had a little outing to Epsom, and that this time you had a decent time. Do you remember the last time we went to Epsom? Since writing you last we have had some awful weather, wet and cold.

The last night we went digging was Wednesday and it poured all the time. We paraded at 6 o'clock and marched up to the line in a perfect downpour. We got back at 3am next morning and found buses waiting to take us to the little village we all disliked so much. We got here at about 5am and had no billets to go to. We were all more or less wet through and tired out. Our bed was the wet ground. Stan and I rigged up a very temporary shelter with our mackintosh capes, which are now not very waterproof and with our groundsheets under us and our greatcoats on, had a good sleep, despite more rain, until nearly midday. Stan's company is quite near us so he and I are living together. On Thursday afternoon we built a more substantial structure with "wattle" walls, made by driving stakes into the ground and hurdling with twigs and branches. The roof is made of two groundsheets and we lay on our capes with our coats to cover us. We sleep very snugly, but it has rained nearly all the time we have been here. Yesterday it rained the whole day and we had a bath parade to a mine some two miles off and got wet through again. Our trouble is that we cannot dry our things. We just sleep in them and the warmth of our bodies dries them. We are in a little wood. Very pretty but frightfully muddy.

We have not had much chance to write letters and the accommodation is very limited.

I suppose you have seen in the papers that the Valuation staff has been reduced. Mallet writes to me that he and many others have received "notice" but that the fellows at the front are "alright".

I shall write to the boss and find out all about it. I am quite well and we are all in the best of spirits altho' yesterday, when they got us wet through to give us a bath was the limit and we all got a bit fed up. This morning, except for a heavy shower, it is fine and our spirits returned.

I got the enclosed letter from a French sergeant of artillery I met at one place we were at and to whom I have occasionally sent a field card. He is a lawyer, and when I last saw him he could not speak English even as well as in his letter, and my French was as bad; yet we got on quite well. He could speak German and that helped a bit. It is quite a souvenir though. Is it not?

Now, my dear, forgive me for not writing before but you know I have been thinking of you all the time.

With all my love, dearest, Ever yours, Ted

P.S. The leave gives us five clear days at home. The translation of this little note is that he is as well as he was at Brébis but the country is better where he now is. "Schowels" are shells. It appears that bombs were dropped on the village where he is camping, but they did not hit the right mark and did no damage.

No. 66 — 6 September 1915

I have received your letter of the 1st and thank you for it. You and Grace seem to have had quite a jolly little dinner party and you seem to have enjoyed it. I am so glad you have a little variation.

We have moved from our bivouac. On Saturday evening we packed up and moved into quite a large town just full of troops. We found billets after a rather long wait. I and my section were lucky and I slept in a bed, the first I believe, since I landed here. It was not a very grand bed but I slept as if in an eider down. We moved again on Sunday at short notice to the mining village we are now in (the same as we were in about a week ago). Again I got a good billet. The platoon sergeant, myself, two lance corporals and Bob Hapgood are billeted here in a miner's cottage and we have two double beds and a single all in one room at our disposal. These are some beds – spotlessly clean and as soft as can be – and last night was the most comfortable I have ever spent or so it seemed.

We were roused up early this morning and were digging just behind the lines all day. This evening I got a little swim in the condensor at the mine.

I hope you are still quite well. I am quite fit and Stan and Charlie are well.

The enclosed snap, which, I think is one which reveals nothing at all of an official nature, depicts three of us after we had secured some wood in a wrecked mine when we were, some time ago, building dugouts. I am some distance behind the chap in the foreground which makes me look rather thin, especially as I am "caught" sideways. He is an artist who has done some good work in sketching the enemy's positions from observation posts. He had also done some fine pictures of various scenes out here. The other chap is a lance corporal pal of mine in my section. Both are Old Dunstonians.

There is nothing more in the way of news and I must soon be going to bed. (It is bed this time, but I am afraid it is a luxury which will not last long.)

Now, dearest, you know all I would say; how I just want you. I wish I could kiss you good night. I do in spirit. Good night, beloved.

No. 67 **8 September 1915**

Thanks for the letter of the 3rd. I cannot tell what has happened to the letter in which I described our Divisional Sports. It was a long one, I believe about eight pages. Have you got it yet? If not I shall have to tell you about them again. I believe I also described therein a Church service held one Saturday evening by the Bishop of Khartoum.

We lost the tug of war.

The weather has improved again and we are still at our old (by now) pastime of digging. It is good exercise. I had a swim in a mine condensor last evening and the evening before and intend to have another today. I am still quite well as is also Stan, Charlie and Leo. I had a letter from Reggie some days ago and he sent his congratulations to you and me. He and Marion are not properly engaged yet but are practically so.

I also had a letter from Cooper at the office. This is an extract: "It was one of the finest things you ever did when you joined the army as you will be as safe as houses as far as this (valuation) job goes. . . . Ridewood has got his commission in the Welsh Borderers . . . and if 'swank' is one of the essential qualities of an officer he will soon reach the pinnacle of fame."

The latter part may or may not interest you.

When next you send a parcel, please include a pair of good strong leather boot laces and I should like some Players Mixture for a change of smoke. The rest I leave entirely to you. I know it will be good.

Once again, my dear, a loving au revoir.

Yours ever, Ted

P.S. Another move on tonight.

No. 68 **9 September 1915**

I am quite well.

I have received your letter dated 6 September 1915.

Letter follows at first opportunity.

Ted

No. 69 **13 September 1915**

Thanks for your letter of the 8th. I am so glad you had a nice time with Evelyn at Pinner.

Fancy an air raid so near home! It will just give you some idea of what a small bombardment is like. Imagine it multiplied by about 4 and seemingly all round your ears and you will know why, after a few days continuance, fellows' nerves begin to suffer.

We had an anti-aircraft gun just outside our billet the other day, they do make quite a noise, don't they – for a little gun?

You had quite a little excitement. I am surprised that you felt safer in the street than the house. The house is the safer; if a bomb drops in the street fragments will not penetrate walls or roof and it it is long odds against them dropping a bomb on one particular house. I do hope it did not upset you too much.

It's another added to a big score we are pledged to wipe out when a chance comes.

You seem to have an idea that we are in the line again but we are not. We only go up there on parties at night time and return to our billets just behind for the day. We came farther back last night and expect to stay here for a few days. I have been awfully busy these last few days, except for a few minutes. I have no spare time. I am doing the combined jobs of orderly sergeant and corporal for the company.

You always want me to suggest something for you to send. May I suggest a tin of Ideal Cream. It is jolly good with fruit.

I trust the Huns have not been dropping any more bombs in or around our neighbourhood and that you, my dear, are quite well. I am.

You know how much I want you, don't you? I just go on living for the time when we shall be reunited. It will not be very long now I think and I go on cheerfully in that thought.

Au revoir my darling. With all my love.

Yours ever, Ted

The Saint

That indiscriminating orb, the moon, gives Private Scattergood a saintly appearance, sadly out of keeping with his thoughts. He's filling 100 sandbags at 11 p.m.

See Letter No. 69

From *Fragments from France* – Bruce Bairnsfather.

Footnote to No. 69:
A Zeppelin raid on London on 8 September caused 106 civilian casualties.

No. 70 [Noeux-les-Mines] 15 September 1915

Thanks for your Sunday letter and for the cake; the two arrived this afternoon. The latter was cut at tea time and we all declared it was good. It must have taken you a long time. It looked so nice in the box and although the top had not got broken it was evident that it had had a rough passage. The cake part underneath just would not stay in whole slices but that made little difference to the fine flavour and its enjoyment. It was jolly well packed. Our company is left in this town while the rest of the batt. is up digging, but we get plenty to do. We had a route march this afternoon and we spent the morning drilling.

I am quite well and I hope you are.

There is absolutely nothing to write about, except that we have found a place where we can have a good meal cooked. We buy the meat at a Butcher's shop (one of the boasts of the town) and the old woman cooks it for us.

We had a feed last night and another is arranged for tonight.

I am, of course, still looking forward to the time when I shall be able to see you.

Au revoir, my dear. With all my love.

Yours, Ted

No. 71 18 September 1915

Thanks for your letters of the 12th and 14th. Do not get hopeless, my dear, all will be well one day.

I am afraid I did not dwell very long on the merits of your splendid cake. It was very nice really. Glad you liked the little picture. I have seen another and I think you can get a copy by mentioning a number to Messrs. Butcher Curnow & Co. the camera people in Blackheath. I will let you know if that is so and what reference to quote.

The bayonet which Spencer took home is a French one – not German. I hope to get one, though. Have you got the grenade yet?

Do not worry your dear little head about the winter. It is not here yet, in fact the weather is topping. A bit too hot, perhaps for work but nice for a swim, when possible. I had one this morning in a mine condensor. There are not so many as you think getting leave, but Bob says that when my turn comes, as it probably will be before his, I have to come and meet you and Elsie Smith and take you both out to tea, at least once so that she can get some news first hand. I don't know whether she would agree to this proposal.

I am still quite well and I hope you and yours are.

Stan and Charlie are both fit. I have not seen Leo for some time, he is away with the machine gun section.

I shall miss the post if I write much more, so au revoir once more.

With all my love. Ever yours, Ted

No. 72 — 21 September 1915

Thanks for letter of the 16th and the parcel. It was a jolly nice one this time. We are back a bit again and in a nice billet where we can get a decent meal and I have another bed, not a very grand one but Bob and I share it and it is better than the floor. He is a kicker and he sneaks all the clothes, but I console myself with the fact that it is a treat to have clothes to be sneaked.

You will wonder why I have not written a letter but I have been so busy. Our platoon officer is away in hospital, sick and the platoon sergeant has been home on a few days leave. His was curtailed owing to stoppage of leave for a while. During his absence I have been in sole charge and have had my hands full. My turn is getting near now, as soon as they start again.

Charlie is quite fit, also Stan and myself. We are in a town with shops and so on and our billet is the scene of a miniature banquet each evening. We came here in motor buses at about four or five o'clock in the morning after a night's digging in advanced trenches. We have plenty of marching and field exercises, just as we did at St. Albans.

I hear that the village we were in last has been badly shelled today.

Thanks for remembrance from Nellie.

So you have decided on Eastbourne for your holiday. I do hope you will have a good time and realize what a fine place it is. I hope the war hasn't made too great a difference to the town. Let me have your address early so that I can write to you there, before you actually go.

There is nothing in the news line that I may put in so I can find very little to "fill up" with. There is of course much that I hope to, one day, tell you but it can't all be put in a letter. You know I love you and am just longing to be near you.

Au revoir again. With all my love, Ted

No. 73 — 24 September 1915

Thanks so much for your letter of the 19th. You want to know what I thought when I first opened the parcel containing the cake? Well I first thought what a brick you were to take such a lot of trouble and then I thought how nice it looked. I thought of course of our wedding cake and birthday cakes.

It is an awful nuisance about the dog so nearly spoiling your holiday. I hope you will be able to go with Grace. It will not be good for you to go down into the country away from home by yourself. Thanks for "reserving" me five days. They will be a holiday when the time comes round.

You had a nice ramble round with your friend. Did it not remind you of little outings like that, which we sometimes had together?

I saw Charlie last night. He is quite well and Stan as well. I haven't seen Leo for quite a long time but I hear he is well.

Will you please post the enclosed for me. I have only one green envelope and we are allowed to send only one other letter and that I have sent home.

I know, darling, that your thoughts are with me wherever I go and I assure you that I think constantly of you. You have all my love and I just long for an opportunity to clasp you in one long embrace.

We are moving up to the line today, sometime, and as I promised to let you know as much as I could, before we parted at St. Albans, I am telling you now what I should otherwise have held back. There is a bit of a scrap coming off and we have the nut to crack. Do not worry if you do not hear for a day or two. I will let you know how I am at first opportunity.

We are in the best of spirits and full of confidence.

Au revoir, my beloved. Yours ever, Ted

Footnote to No. 73:
This letter was written on the eve of the Battle of Loos in which the 20th. was to play a conspicuous part.

Happy Memories of the Zoo
"What time do they Feed the Sea-Lions, Alf?"

See Letter No. 81

From *Fragments from France* – Bruce Bairnsfather.

OCTOBER 1915.

Major E. H. Norman was transferred out to command the 17th. London on 2 October and in his place Lieutenant C. W. Clout[1] was appointed Adjutant of the 20th. The next day, Sunday, a Brigade Church Parade was held after which the troops were addressed and complimented on their recent work by Major General Sir C. Barter KCB, CVO the General Officer Commanding 47th. Division.

The first fortnight of October was spent in re-training the battalion and in absorbing replacements after the losses at Loos. Five new officers joined on 5 October (2nd Lieutenants Elliott, Glascodine, Mackie, Robertson and Weston) and three more on the 11th (2nd Lieutenants Crawford, Dilke and Terry). Brigade route marches and field exercises were held and practice in open order drill and the taking up of artillery formation from column of route. On 9 October, Lieutenant General Sir Henry Rawlinson, G.O.C. IV Army Corps, inspected 141 and 142 Brigades, complimenting them on their appearance and their work.

The 20th. returned towards the firing line on 12 October moving to billets in Mazingarbe where they remained the following day in reserve to an attack by the 1st. Division on the front opposite Hulluch. The day after the attack the 47th. Division relieved the 1st., the 20th. London taking over the front line from the South Wales Borderers in trenches along the north-east and south-east sides of the copse near the Bois Carré west of the Loos-La Bassée road. Battalion HQ was in a nearby chalk pit. Parts of the line were already in very bad condition and four days of artillery activity in bad weather, did not improve matters. The months of October and November were unusually wet. 2nd Lieutenant Robertson was killed on 18 October; the following day working parties from the 4th. Royal Welsh Fusiliers began to construct a new front line across the re-entry in the right centre of the battalion front, which was immediately occupied by 'C' Coy. The Battalion War Diary records "furious activity" on 22 October with continuous shelling; a smoke-bomb dump close to Battalion HQ, was set on fire and a new German battery did a lot of damage to 'C' Coy's lines – both the old and the newly dug.

After dusk on 23 October the London Irish relieved the 20th. who moved back into the former German second line which with continuous rain became ankle-deep with water. For four days the battalion's main task was the reconstruction of trenches extending north of the chalk pit; it was hampered by heavy rain and frequent artillery duels.

Footnote:
1. C. W. Clout was an Old Boy of the Roan School, Greenwich.

Eventually relieved by the 7th. London, the 20th. returned by the slow route via Lone Tree to billets in Mazingarbe, but after only 24 hours, 'C' Company had to go forward again to assist the 18th. London in the four keeps of the former German front line.

No. 74 **1 October 1915**

Dearest,

At last I have an opportunity to write more than a service card. We are at present out of range of the guns. We took part in the great attack on Saturday morning last, but as regards time it might be a few minutes ago or years. One loses absolutely all reckoning of time. This battalion advanced two miles, pushing the Germans back and capturing hundreds of prisoners and two field guns. We consolidated our position and dug ourselves in, under fire and held on for four days and nights. During that time it was one long strain, standing to to repel counter attacks all day and all night. We got no sleep and at the end we could scarcely stand, we were that tired. We were relieved in the early hours of Wednesday morning and got a short sleep in some wrecked houses a little way back, from which we moved in the evening to some more wrecked houses where we spent a very cold night. Yesterday morning we expected to go into the fight again but some other troops were in a position to be rushed up quicker and after a "touch and go" interview between our colonel and brigadier, we were sent back for a rest. It was a gruelling march; everyone felt knocked up and when we did reach our billets we slept like tops. I turned in, in a barn on thick straw at about 9 and slept till 8 this morning without moving, I believe. We charged with lightened packs having given in overcoats and capes and having no extra covering than a groundsheet. The weather was most inclement. It rained nearly all the time and was as cold as it could be. We were all wet thro' practically the whole time.

We, of course, lost some men, but not so many as the perfect hail of shells and bullets through which we advanced would have warranted. They were just pounded away at our trench like mad and it seemed as if no one could get out of it unscathed. That half hour or so was the tensest I have ever spent and yet everyone got out when the time came and advanced in great style. I cannot dwell on all the horrors and I am sure you would not like to get too vivid a description. Our losses were most heavy in officers, in proportion. I expect you have heard by now that Charlie got a bullet thro' his shoulder. It was as nice a wound as one could get. He did not know he was wounded for some time and I expect he is in England by now. Leo was badly hit and I am afraid I have lost a pal. Bob Hapgood, Stan and I are quite unscathed. This morning we had a speech by the brigadier who congratulated us on our good work and steadiness, but I think we were at the end of our tether when relieved. Leave is stopped for a while but we live in hopes. The morale and spirits of our chaps are splendid and it has proved that the once derided "terriers" are as good soldiers as any.

Your letter of the 23rd is the only one I have received since last Friday and that came on the last day in the trench. It was good to get it. It reminded me of home and all we had to fight for. No more at present, you know I want more than ever to see you and tell you how I love you. Au revoir my own girlie.

With all my love. Yours, Ted

P.S. Two souvenirs of the Bosches. I have a bayonet to make a pair with the other, this time a German one.

Footnote to No. 74:
This letter also contained two epaulettes torn from german uniforms, with coloured piping and regimental numbers – one in red, the other yellow.

No. 75 — 3 October 1915

I hardly know what to write about. I could fill pages about the affair which seems now like a nightmare but I would not burden you or worry you with all the harrowing details. It is Sunday today and although the preceding night was cold, this morning is bright and sunny – a pleasant change. We are to have blankets tonight, so we shall sleep warmer.

Thanks so much for your letter of 29th ult. and the dear little photo. I think it is topping and I prize it very much. I wish I could get more snapshots of people and things that happen at home. Couldn't you do something with my camera? I suppose you have now heard all details about Charlie. There is no need to worry. We all consider he was very lucky as we presume he is in England by now.

Please congratulate your Dad on passing successfully in his Exam.

I hope you have heard by now that Alec is well again.

I hear that Elsie Smith was trying to persuade you to attend some cookery classes. It would make something to do in the evenings. What?

Now my dear, I must again say "au revoir".

With all my love. Yours ever, Ted

Footnote to No. 75:
Charles Randall had enlisted in the British Red Cross and had started voluntary hospital work.

No. 76 — 6 October 1915

Thanks for your letter of the 1st. It is the only one, except the ones I have already acknowledged, I have received lately and your parcel has not yet shown up. It is still raining and mud is now the prominent feature of this part of the world. I hope that the weather is more favourable with you by the "briny".

I hope your anxiety is now set at rest by at least one of the several letters I have written.

I hope you will like Herne Bay. One chap in my section used to live there and he thinks it is a topping place. Stan and I are still well and I hope that you are too.

There is nothing to write about except that I think we are going to get a bath today. That will be rather a treat. We had a change of underclothes yesterday, not before we wanted it.

This is the last letter I shall write to Herne Bay as they seem to take a long time, so you should find one at home when you get back.

Now, my dear, I must again say au revoir.

With all my love. Ted

No. 77 **9 October 1915**

Thanks for letters of 2nd and an undated one, presumably the 4th and for the parcel, especially the socks. I just did want them.

We had a day of alarms yesterday. We stood by all day, packed up ready to move at a moment's notice and all night too. This morning we were inspected by General Rawlinson who commands our Army Corps.

I got Grace's letter card this morning and from the views I should think Herne Bay is a nice place and above all your anxiety, I hope you had a passable time there.

Glad to see by your little poscript that your Dad has had news of Charlie. I expect fuller details in your next letter. I was not far from him and saw him walking or at least running in pursuit of some Germans, presumably after he was hit. I hear that he did not know until some time after that he had got it. Two chaps in my section were killed and two wounded out of nine, including myself. One of the wounded is on the right, somewhat in the background, of that last little snapshot I sent you. He was not very bad – a piece of bomb in his thigh – but he was plucky. He quickly slit his trouser leg and bound up his wound and came on. He would not go back until I sent him as escort to some prisoners.

I can get no further news of poor old Leo. He is reported badly wounded but I hear unofficially that he died. He lay for some time before he could be moved and I have found the fellows who at some risk carried him down to a dressing station and they say he was brave and was still alive when they left him with the stretcher bearers.

Stan has been made a sergeant as in his company nearly all the sergeants were casualties, but in our platoon, except for appointments of new lance corporals, things are as they were.

I am quite well and I sincerely hope you are. You know, dear, how I think of you. I do wish there were means to set all your fears at rest but I know that it is your love that prompts them. I long just to see you and tell you all about everything.

Au revoir my beloved, Ted

No. 78 — 11 October 1915

You will be pleased to know we are still "resting", behind the line. We have found a very nice little place, where we have rather extravagant little "feeds" in the evenings. I forgot to tell you about it before. We heard some good news from the line last night and as that corresponded with a pay day, we celebrated it with champagne.

We also got a fellow, who is on brigade staff and therefore has opportunity to carry a violin with him, to come in and play us a few selections. He is a fine player and his fiddle almost speaks. He played so well that I and Bob, at least, were quite carried away. He (the violinist – not Bob) played "Nights of Gladness", "Tales of Hoffman", "A Hungarian Air" and "Serenata" among others and it was delightful. I could not help thinking of you.

Thanks for your letter of Wednesday. Would you please send me as soon as possible another watch-guard. You know what I mean – the little hinged cover. If you ask the dealer for "size 3" you will get the size right, and if possible would you get a khaki coloured one instead of shiny. I also want a towel, a pencil and handkerchiefs.

How is Charlie getting on? I hear the sad news that "Dicky" Benwell, another friend in my section has died of wounds. He was such a nice chap too.

Bob showed me a paragraph in a letter he had from Elsie Smith. It was about you and she paid you such a pretty compliment. I should think she must be awfully nice. I have seen her photograph.

I am glad you had such a nice change at Herne Bay. I hope Grace's hat did not suffer too much at the concert. I wish I could have had just a week-end with you there, or anywhere else.

You know how I look forward to the time when I shall be able to enjoy your delightful presence.

Good night, my beloved. Yours ever, Ted

No. 79 — 13 October 1915

Thanks for your letter of the 9th. I am so sorry my letters take so long in transport but that's not my fault. I am so glad that you have such a good "pal" in Grace. I hope you really did forget things for a little while at least.

We made another move last night and are now up in reserve, exactly what for, I don't know, but I think something is on the board. So Charlie is at Eastbourne. It would have been better if he could have spent his convalescence at home, I did not know Mother knew Sergt. Williams. He went home at about half an hour's notice. How exciting! He did not even have time to pack up.

I am afraid my turn will not be just yet as one or two chaps who have lost brothers or relatives are going first in our company. Quite right I think. Don't you?

I wonder if you dreamt I came home on the same night as I met you. I do not know where or why and I did not want to discover that. It was about a week ago and I was so disappointed to find it was only a dream. (It has started to rain and the roof leaks.)

What does Grace think about giving away Jimmy as a mascot?

By the way – have you got my letter with the German epaulettes in it? Thanks for the "Mercury".

I have started to read such a jolly book entitled "Pip". One of the chaps had it sent to him. I hope I shall get a chance to read it before I lose it or have to chuck it away.

Now, Girlie dear, I must again say "au revoir". I can't tell you how I want you in a letter but I am so happy to know that you love me as you do. I am a lucky chap to have such love. I just live to see you and love you.

It is such an incentive to feel that one has all that one holds dear at home safe in England to fight for and keep safe.

With all my love. Ever yours, Ted

P.S. Please post enclosed. Two are for a friend of mine but you won't mind will you? Green envelopes are precious.

No. 80 — 19 October 1915

I was overjoyed to get your letter of the 14th this morning. The last before that was yours of the 9th which came quickly. The interval seemed ages. I just longed to hear from you. We are in very uncomfortable trenches this time. I think it is an old German line converted and the shells have smashed it "some" We have no dugouts and get very little sleep as we have to be continually repairing broken places.

The Germans "straffe" us periodically with artillery and keep us in a state of "qui vive". We miss our old trench parties which used to be quite picnics. There is a bombardment on now just along the line. We had our innings yesterday. I am still quite fit but it is cold at nights and foggy too. This fact (the fog) gets on one's nerves a bit as we cannot see what's going on, but I think it worries the enemy more. To think you have had those horrible "Zeps" over again. I cannot help feeling very indignant.

I suppose Charlie is home by now. Isn't he lucky? Surprised to hear that he didn't like Eastbourne. I should like to see it – lights or no lights – what!

Thanks for the promise of parcel. I am sorry I asked for a towel as I have got a fine new one now (Army issue).

Glad to know mine is a lucky number. All the other chaps say there's (sic) are

Footnote to No. 80:
A Zeppelin raid on London on 13 October caused numerous civilian casualties – 56 killed and 114 injured.

lucky now because some divide by fives, twos, threes, etc. Why is mine lucky? I hope it is dear, for our mutual sakes. Thank Grace for the prophecy. To think Williams hadn't better sense than to start a rumour like that. I got hit on the leg with a piece of brick, when a shell exploded, and got a few days rest in my billet for it. It was months ago.

I dreamt again the other night as I lay in the trench, that I was home with you. I only hope it will not be too long before I am. Once more now au revoir, dearest.

With all my love. Yours, Ted

P.S. Please post enclosed – may only send off these "greens".

No. 81 — 26 October 1915

Thanks for your letters of 17th, 18th, 19th, 21st and 22nd. What a lot to answer at once! At last I have an opportunity of doing so. Thanks for green envelopes and your two parcels. They both came in the trenches to me. The towel was useful after all, as I lost mine. But soap and toothpowder! If you had seen me this morning or any time lately you would have thought I needed them. For twelve days I had not washed or shaved, but this morning I had quite a little bath in a "mess tin".

Since reading "Pip" I have read another book by Ian Hay "A Man's Man" and I thought it jolly good, but really one does not get much chance to read. I read that to detract my thoughts from the shelling to which we were subject one day.

We spent nine days in the front line and had a hot time with the shells. Luckily it was fine for that period, but when we came out into these reserve trenches it rained hard for two days. We have been here three, and are going back to the first line again tonight.

The trench we are in has been up to our ankles in water, and the little shelter I rigged up to sleep in has let the water in on me.

Stan was very lucky to get home when he did. I nearly came with him. Did he tell you about that? Mine was cancelled ten minutes before the time of leaving.

We were out on a working party last night until 2am. It was cold and wet and the mud everywhere! My clothes are a whitish brown instead of khaki.

I am glad Charlie is getting on so well.

I have not seen Guy Bush although we are at the place you say he is.

I expect Stan has been able to tell Charlie all about the numbers he wanted. I mustn't put that in a letter. No. 7 platoon suffered most.

I cannot say when I shall be coming home now. At least a few weeks, I think, before I can go.

Thank your Dad for his letter. I will reply when I get a chance.

Now, my girlie, I must again say au revoir. Oh how I wish I could be just taking you in my arms – muddy even as they are – and telling you how my soul yearns for you.

Your lover, Ted

P.S. So glad you and Elsie Smith get on so well together.

P.S. 27th. Couldn't post this yesterday. Still quite fit. In the front line again. A few shells over this morning.

No. 82 **31 October 1915**

I have again an opportunity of writing you. We are now out of the trenches after a spell of 16 weary days. You say in one of your letters that the nights must seem long but this time it was the days, as the enemy's artillery was quiet most of the night while during the day they kept up an almost continuous bombardment. We used to count the hours to nightfall. We had some rain too and when we were at last relieved it was as much as we could do to stagger along the muddy roads. Despite all that we finished up singing at the tops of our voices. I think for the last few days it was only the rum issue that kept us going. How we slept when we reached our billets, although we had no bed but the floor and our windows were devoid of glass, allowing a liberal supply of "cool" fresh air. This will not be going out today as I have overslept the post. (We did not get in until two this morning).

I cannot remember which of your letters I have acknowledged but I have them all up to the 29th. I got two today. How lucky I am to have your loving letters to cheer me up. I just long to see your writing on the envelopes when the post comes in. We are arranging a little feast tonight with champagne.

1 November 1915

This morning is another wet one. We have just got back from a bath. It was luxurious. We took off our clothes in one part, passed on into the compartment with rows of tubs of hot water, bathed and passed into the dressing room. Our clothes which were labelled like a cloakroom had in the meantime been ironed (to rid them of vermin) and brushed and we were served out with clean underclothes. We emerged clean. It was like a human laundry machine. In one side dirty. Out the other clean. The whole establishment is a converted brewery.

Bob and I thought of you on Thursday evening. We sat under our groundsheets, with the rain pouring down and tried to imagine what you and Elsie Smith were doing. He and I have been together all the time in the same fire bay, if that conveys anything.

Thanks so much for the leaflet of the service at St. Mary's. It must have been very impressive.

What happened to Charlie when he reported to Tadworth Depot?

Stan and I are going to apply for commissions in the R.E.s (Engineers) at present in England and as we, if successful, have to spend a period in training in England I think it a good idea.

The lot we are trying to get into and in which Stan has a friend who will recommend us to the Colonel, do road-making etc. behind the line and I think that after the share of trenches we have had, a change will be good. What do you think?

I don't know when my leave will come off but I hope within a month.

Now, darling, I must close and once more wish you a loving "au revoir". You have my love.

Yours. Ted

P.S. Kindest regards to Charlie and your Dad.

At the Brewery Baths

"You chuck another sardine at me, my lad, and you'll hear from my solicitors"

See Letter No. 82 From *Fragments from France* – Bruce Bairnsfather.

NOVEMBER – DECEMBER 1915

The first twelve days of November were very wet and front line activity was restricted. On 2 November Lieutenant Colonel A. B. Hubback of the 20th. took temporary command of 141 Brigade during the absence of General Thwaites and Captain E. J. Dolphin commanded the 20th. The Lord Mayor of London inspected 141 Brigade on 6 November.

Sunday 7 November found the 20th. once more back in the front line with the 18th. on their left and 140 Brigade on their right. As a result of the rain, trenches and dugouts were in danger of collapsing. After being relieved by the 17th London on 10 November, the battalion moved into the old German reserve line in "Fourth Avenue" where Captain Stanger was killed by a "Pipsqueak". The night of 12 November found working parties trying to clear mud and water from Vendin Allée; but the 20th. was relieved by the Loyal North Lancashire Regiment the following night and returned to billets in Mazingarbe by 01.00 hours on 14 November. This was the beginning of one month's respite for the 20th. – the 47th. Division was replaced by the 1st. for a period of rest and training in the Lillers area. The 20th. travelled by train from Noeux-les-Mines to Lillers where they were billeted overnight before going on to Rimbert which was to house them for a week. Route marches made the battalion a familiar sight on the roads between Ferfay, Burbure, Allouagne, Lozinghem, Marles-les-Mines, Auchel and district. During this time Lieutenant Colonel Hubback returned to resume command of the battalion with Major H. Campbell (attached from 13th London) as his 2 i/c; four new officers were gazetted as 2/lieuts. on promotion from the ranks: CSM Read, M. S., Sergeant Lane, M., Sergeant Lomas, G., Sergeant Burt, E. G. All four had sailed for France with the Battalion on 9 March.

Some 150 men attended a Church Parade on Sunday 21 November and the following evening about 100 officers and men were entertained by "The Follies" – the 47th. Divisional Concert Party – in Lillers.

At the end of the second week of December 1915 the 47th. Division relieved the 15th. in the northern sector of the Loos salient including the quarries and the Hohenzollern Redoubt in front of Hulluch. The ensuing period was one of static trench warfare hampered by the winter weather. The war diary of the 20th. has been lost for the days between 3 December and 1 January, but the now customary routine for the front line troops continued. Ted Trafford missed one week of this as he was lucky enough to be granted his long-awaited home leave (5 days at home with 1 day each way for travelling) in mid-December 1915.

No. 83 **3 November 1915**

My dearest,

I have just received your letter of the 31st ult. You cannot know how I feel about you being left so long without a letter. I feel so powerless to alleviate your anxiety, when I have no chance to write you more than a field p.c.

Stan and I have filled in our commission papers and have passed the necessary medical examination. We are putting them in for signature by the Colonel and Brigadier.

It has done me in the eye for another stripe, I think. The weather which has been so wretched is a bit brighter today, except for an early morning fog and I only hope the improvement will last a little while. Stan's company are going up the line today, manning a keep for 24 hours. I don't know if we shall get a turn.

I am still quite well and I hope you and yours are.

Charlie is, as you say, very lucky. I suppose his shoulder won't permit him to carry a pack. Eh? I hope he is quite well otherwise.

I wish I could do something to cheer you up a bit – you seem so lonely. How I wish I could take you in my arms and make you oh! so happy. I just long for that opportunity.

I do hope for your sake that my leave will soon be granted. I shall call at your place first, on my way home and you shall come home to "brekka" with me. What a spell of happiness we shall be able to make that all-too-short week!

Apropos your P.S. about dear old Leo. The official report is "wounded" and that is all his father will believe but I know he died because a stretcher bearer, who was with him at the last, told me. It is a terrible business.

Now, Girlie dear, I can find nothing more to write about. You know I love and think of you all the while.

Au revoir, beloved. Yours, Ted

P.S. Please send a few pipe-cleaners and bachelor buttons.

No. 84 **5 November 1915**

Thanks so much for your letter of the 1st. It arrived last night. I was so pleased to know that you had at last got more than a field card.

We are still back, but send up working parties to the line each night. I have not had to go on one yet. I am on Brigade Guard today, until noon tomorrow. We have quite a comfy little guard room, stone floor and windows without glass, but weatherproof, with a large brazier and plenty of coke. The place is full of smoke but warm and we have been busy warming up some stew adding Oxo and preparing "welsh rarebit", toast, tea etc. We look like having a good time.

It is a cold but fine night and I have only to go out to relieve the sentries and visit them. It means keeping awake all night so I shall be thinking of you during my lonely vigil among the snoring reliefs. There is is a rumour that we are going up the line again very soon – I don't know how true it is. There is also a rumour of more leave in the near future. Hope on with me.

Thank Charlie for his letter. I will reply later on. Give him a Cheer Ho! from me. You ask me about my pals. Well, there was a little "clique" of which I was part but it is sadly depleted. At present there is Sergeant Mortleman (Sonny), Bob Hapgood, Sergeant Burt (Niffy) and Frank Storch (the platoon dandy). There was Billie Barclay, now home wounded, "Dicky" Benwell, now "died of wounds", Freddie Goosey and his brother Gerald, who was killed in action. Fred went on leave when I so nearly did and has seen an army doctor in England and been posted to Home Service as unfit for foreign service. There was also poor old "Delts" Dangerfield and Roland Knight, both now killed.

Of those left, now that poor old Leo is gone, my special chums, besides Stan, are Bob and Storch. I hope for an opportunity soon to be able to tell you all about everybody. Storch is an awfully nice chap and when he goes on leave, he says he will call on you. He knows you well. Having seen several photos of you and hearing a good deal about you. He also is engaged to a girl in Yorkshire. Did you see the photograph in the illustrated papers two days ago of Captain Escombe's wedding?

There is nothing more to write about at present, so Good-night my dear.

With all my love. Ted

No. 85 — 9 November 1915

Thanks so much for your letters of 3rd, 5th, and 6th. The two latter arrived together last night, together with the Mercury. Also many thanks for the parcel. It has been most useful. A parcel of good things when in the trenches is most useful. It arrived just as we were marching off and although I am afraid I grumbled at having to carry it when already loaded, when I opened it, I was fully recompensed. We have enjoyed it all immensely. It was an awful journey up here with mud up to our boot tops. Thank Charlie for his very welcome contribution. Tell him we have no dug-outs. I hope you are keeping fit; Stan and I are.

I had a letter from Harry in which he tells me that Leo Howard's mother died suddenly last week. Poor old Leo. I am sorry for him.

I am afraid I must make this a short letter or I shall miss the post.

You know all I would say. How I just long for you. I am almost sure to be home within a fortnight.

Au revoir, my beloved. With all my love, Yours, Ted

P.S. Glad you had a "cosy" week-end with Elsie.

No. 86 [Rimbert] **14 November 1915**

Thanks for your letter of 9th. We are now out of the firing line and quite a long way back for a rest period. We were relieved on Saturday night and made a slow journey, owing to mud, shell holes etc. back to a village and got to our billets (ours was a barn) at about 1 a.m. where we slept. Next day we went farther back; starting about midday and marching part and riding in a train the rest, to a central town quite a large place [Lillers], where I had walked to some months ago when we were back. We spent the night here and had a grand feast in the evening. We left there early the next morning and came here after about a three miles march. We have not been here before but have marched through it. We were billeted in a loft, overrun with rats and none too clean while the roof looked as if it leaked badly. It was not good enough if we were to be here any time so we billeted ourselves (Bob acting as interpreter) after getting permission. We have now a topping little place in a cottage where we have a little room between the four (Bob, Storch, Sonny and I). We have chairs and a little table and use of the living room and table for meals. The good woman, whose husband is at the War, cooks for us and makes us very comfortable. We had a fine little dinner today and now tonight she has let us use her table and lamp to write. I have had time to write before but the letter could not have gone off while we were on the move. Thanks for starting more socks. Would it be too much to ask you to make a pair with long legs up to below the knee. In fact, if possible I should like any more you do to be like that. Now dearest, it is time for lights out and we must soon be turning in. The only drawback to this place is the floor of tiles for sleeping on but with a groundsheet and greatcoat underneath and a blanket over we should be warm if we squeeze together. The room is fine and warm now. I must look round for some sacks of straw for palliasses. We have put up our photographs on the little sideboard in our room, yours, Elsie Smith's and Storch's girl's so we can be reminded of you often if it be necessary. Now my dear I shall go to sleep thinking of you.

Good-night, my beloved, Ted

15 November 1915

Good morning, my girlie, I hope you are well. I am. We have spent a good night and slept well and warmly. There is snow on the ground this morning. Not much, and it looks so pretty. It seems warmer too as there is no wind, although it was 'fresh' washing at the pump. I forgot to tell you of the three little kiddies here. They are topping little boys and have taken a great fancy to us or our army jam.

Now dearest, au revoir. I think the leave must soon come now.

With all my love. Yours, Ted

P.S. Your letter of 11th just to hand. Thanks! Will reply later on.

No. 87 — 17 November 1915

I cannot make out what has happened to your letters. I should surely have got another tonight, but I haven't. It may turn up tomorrow.

There is nothing in the way of news, except that Stan and I are quite well. We are very comfortable in our billet. The people in this town are the most hospitable we have yet come across. Glad you like the cookery class. It makes a change, doesn't it? The leave seems nearer now but they are sending privates now and my turn will not be for a few days; it will probably be within the next two weeks.

So Charlie is recruiting! I hope their efforts will bring better fruit than those fellows who recruited the third battalion drafts we have had. They are mostly boys or chaps who joined the third thinking they would not be out here yet. There is a great difference between them and the remnant of "the old guard".

You say I have to have a photo' taken. I should look fine with my hair short – like a jailbird who has been liberated for a couple of weeks.

Our commission papers have been signed by the C.O. and been sent through to Brigade H.Q. It may be a long time before anything happens. The machinery of the important "heads" works slowly except in the cases of wrongdoers. I had a letter from Cecil Durrant. He is out here in the Wiltshires and has been to several places where we have been entrenched.

Now, dear, "nil desperandum". Hope on. We shall be so happy one day in each other's love. I am looking forward so earnestly to seeing you and to have the opportunity of buying you your Christmas gift.

Once more then, au revoir my beloved.

With all my love. Yours, Ted

P.S. Please post enclosed.

No. 88 — 19 November 1915

Thanks so much for your letters of the 14th and 16th which arrived last night and today respectively.

We are still having a fairly good time in our billet and living well too, although we spend a good deal of time on parade. Stan and I with other N.C.O.s have been detailed as instructors on a recruits' ground for the new drafts. What does Charlie think of that? It's like the old Hatfield days. Of course it only lasts while we are here. You think your letters do not do much to cheer me but I assure you they are what I look forward to more than anything else. On Sunday night when you wondered where I was when you heard the windows rattling I was quite comfy in Lillers. When you saw our guns did it occur to you that Stan and I actually touched them?

How is Elsie Phillips? Has she heard lately from Will? I have enquired about him from men of his battalion but no one seems to know him. Glad you had a nice evening with her. I wish I could have seen you home. Did I tell you about our feed in the trenches? Bob had a fowl, roasted and cold sent out. We soon made short work of that, and Sonny had a plum pudding while "Storchy" had fruit and cream. What do you think of that? We had roast leg of mutton yesterday and two veg. It has been cold today but I have not noticed it much. Getting used to it and being well wrapped up, I suppose.

Now dearest, Good night!

Heaps of Love. Ever yours, Ted

Footnote to No. 88:
The reference to "our guns" concerns the two German field guns captured by the 20th. in the chalk-pit at Loos. With other war trophies they were displayed on Horse Guards Parade in London.

No. 89 — Dated by Ted 22/9/15 (a slip of the pen) but postmarked 25 November

Thanks so much for your letter of Friday last. I should have written yesterday but I had not received your letter then and I did not feel like writing, although I was in the best of spirits, besides I heard a rumour that I was to go on leave today but nothing has come of that. I think, however, that it is only a matter of days now. We work pretty hard on the drill ground all day long and it's pretty cold for that kind of game, but I have kept quite warm so far.

Yesterday, being Sunday, for once in a way we had a complete rest and I scarcely left the billet all day. I did not even put my boots on. The first day since we landed that I have enjoyed such a luxury. I now am the proud possessor of a pair of slippers – we all have them in our house, quite cheap canvas ones with hemp soles – bought at the village stores, but they are nice for the evenings. We only go out for parades and small errands as we are so cosy. We spend the evenings, reading, writing, playing whist etc. or doing small odd jobs.

We had quite a Sunday dinner yesterday. The good lady got us and cooked for us a loin of pork and potatoes and onions. We made some soup with Foster Clarks tablets and for dessert we had tinned peaches. For supper we make Quaker Oats which are obtainable here.

I am sorry to hear about poor old Alec having such a thin time. I do hope he is now on his way to recovery.

Today was a proper arctic freezer. It was freezing until nearly noon and there was a slight fog. As we walked about, ice formed on our clothing but it was warmer, so long as one kept moving, than it is when the piercing wind blows as it often does.

Now, darling, I really do not think it will be long before I can see you and take you in my arms and tell you all I would say and all about everything. If only it were to be tomorrow – What bliss!

There is a concert tonight at .... by "The Follies" or at least half is by them and half by talented soldiers. We could not all go as there were buses or lorries to convey those going and they could not carry the whole battalion. We "drew" for it and I was not lucky. It is as well, perhaps, or I should have had to write a shorter letter.

Once more then, au revoir, for a short while, I hope.

With all my love, Ted

No. 90 **25 November 1915**

Thanks for Sunday's letter. We are still in our comfortable billet, but I think we are all four feeling somewhat fed up with things. I should have written last evening but there was a reorganisation of our company which caused some excitement and not a small sensation. Whether the cause was that four "pals" were altogether whom the powers that be thought should be separated, or whether the separation is only the effect of some other cause I do not know, but the result is the same. Four of us, "Sonny", Frank, Bob and myself have been together through the whole of the campaign and I think our comradeship has served us in good stead in several "hot" times. It has never made us neglect duty but we are all now in different platoons. I am in No. 5, but we still hope to see a good deal of each other. Of course, in other platoons little friendships have been broken up in this way. I suppose we must just grin and bear it. We can do nothing.

Sergeants Burt, Lane, Lomas DCM and CSM Read have all been promoted to 2nd Lieuts. in this battalion. Charlie will remember the names.

I don't know when we shall hear any more about our commissions (Stan's and mine). We have to supply birth certificates now and we are waiting for a nomination from our prospective new C.O.

I think my leave is actually due in a week's time. I hope nothing crops up to alter it.

There is nothing more to write about now. You know all I would say. You know how I just long to see you and tell you all about everything.

Au revoir, I'll see you soon. With all my love, Ted

No. 91 **28 November 1915**

Thanks so much for your letter of 23rd which arrived on Friday evening. It is now Sunday morning and you will think I should have answered before, but Saturday was a busy day and after parades I had a little tea party for which your parcel arrived just in time. The whole thing was very nice. The little cakes, the cake, the chocolates and the cigars were all thoroughly appreciated. The cigars were voted excellent and speak well for Charlie's choice. Do not think that in entertaining my friends out here I forgot you. I only thought how nice it would have been if you and I could have spent the day together, but thanks so much for the parcel which helped to remind me it was my birthday. I hope you won't think we were too despondent when you read my last letter. I wrote it as I did so that the officer who censored it could see how we felt about it and perhaps I "piled it on". You might tell my people that, will you? I haven't another green envelope. We are still together in our billet but expect we shall be separated when we move. Bob and Frank are both lance corporals now.

I hope your headache and cold are better now. We are getting some very cold weather now but it is a dry cold and can be contended with. We have been served out with leather jerkins, a kind of long sleeveless waistcoat made of leather lined with cloth, which keeps the wind out. By this time next week I shall know definitely about my leave and shall, I expect, be getting ready to go on the Tuesday.

Now dearest, I shall soon be telling you all about it all. So once more, au revoir.

With all my love, Ted

P.S. Please thank your Dad for his letter it was nice of him to remember the date.

P.S.S. I heard from Will James last night. He is still well. We occasionally exchange field cards.

No. 92 **3 December 1915**

I expect you wonder at the gap in my correspondence but I will explain; on Tuesday we were to start on a three days' 'trek' but as the weather was so inclement it was postponed until the next day. We were of course very busy all day Tuesday and were "standing by" all day so I could not settle down to write. Eventually we started away on Wednesday morning after a 5 o'clock reveille. It was pouring when we started but cleared up during the morning. It was a divisional turn out and, as Charlie will tell you, to take part in a march of the whole division is a tiresome affair. The packs were like those we carried from Hardifort (Charlie will explain), the leather jerkins taking the place of skin coats. Unfortunately I got sore feet. The first time they have been properly blistered, owing to my own boots being at the regimental shoemaker's and my having to wear some second hand ones he lent me, while my own were being repaired, which were far too big for me and slipped and rubbed my "tootsies". We did a full fifteen miles the first day and then there was some outpost practice. We were lucky not to get outpost duty at night as it rained the whole time and the battalion that did have to do it must have had a rough time. Our billet for the night was a barn in which we were quite comfy; as a matter of fact I and three other NCOs slept on the floor of the farmhouse adjoining. Next day we came back, that was yesterday, and my feet were still "crocked" but I stuck it for a long while as I don't like falling out on a march. When about 7 miles away, the captain, a new man named Ward from South Africa, said he would like to walk and if I liked I could ride his horse. I accepted his offer and came home in great style mounted for the first time, some swank! What! My feet are much better today and when I get my own boots back I shall be A.1 again. I shall be off parade until I get them. Now, having explained what I have been doing instead of writing you I will proceed to answer your letters of the 25th, 28th and 30th. One reached me on Tuesday night, one on Wednesday and one today. I hope you have not worried at all because you have not heard. I thought of you all the time as I nearly always do. You mentioned that you had been making some cheese biscuits – strange but that day "Sonny" had a parcel with some in. They are topping! I have given Bob a good talking to because Elsie Smith has not been turning up to cookery.

That helmet! I had quite forgotten that I had not written an acknowledgement. It arrived while I was in the trenches and one of the field p.c.s referred to its receipt. It is a nice warm one. Thanks very much. Your Dad had a busy day at the hospital. He is as ever a busy man and is now doing "his bit" as much as we.

You seem to think I was very disappointed about that concert. I wasn't! It would have been a cold journey and we had a good evening indoors as usual since we have been here. We had a good "grub" yesterday evening when we got in after bathing our feet and ourselves – Pork chops, fried potatoes, champagne, cigars and Xmas pudding, the two latter articles coming from England in parcels. I get on quite well with the youngsters here, especially the youngest who calls me "camalard" for comrade. He doesn't understand much I say to him even when I "speak" or stammer French and I know very little of what he actually intends to say but we seem to understand and get on first rate.

I do not know what to say to you to make matters better for you at home. I know, dearest, that you have a thin time through your aunt and that from that quarter you have little sympathy ever, but you know well that I extend you all the sympathy and love of which I am capable. I wish I were in a position to take you out of it all. When I come home I shall just make you forget it for a while and when this wretched war is over I will make up to you for it all. I will strive my hardest to get quickly into a position which will allow us to marry and then although I do not suppose our troubles will be entirely over we can share them and that will make them easier. I am so sorry you are unhappy at home and I feel so helpless to do anything for you. You will be happier, won't you? – when I come and put my arms round you next week. I shall just kiss all your troubles away. I am glad you told me about it. Troubles bring us closer.

Thanks for remembrances from "New York Nellie".

We are still waiting for a letter of nomination from the CO of the Engineers and until that arrives we can do nothing further.

Now dear, I must close and for a little longer it must be au revoir. I have heaps of letters to write to Mallet, Harry, Les, Reg, Will, Mother, Harold and Nellie Davis from all of whom I have received letters lately which still remain unanswered.

Good night, my beloved. Yours ever, Ted

P.S. Please post enclosed for my chum "Sonny".

No. 93 **5 December 1915**

Thanks for your letter of the 2nd just received. There is really so little to write about that I feel almost at a loss. Nothing exciting happens here. On Friday we had a bath parade and it rained practically all day. Yesterday it still rained but we went to the range – a small one which was hastily improvised – to put some of the new draft men through some firing practice. I got wet through and incidentally won a small sweepstake which the NCOs on the range organised and competed in. On Saturday evening we had a brigade concert in the local school and it turned out a great success. All the artistes were in the brigade and most were in this battalion.

There was an orchestra consisting of piano, flute, two violins, three mandolines and a small drum. They performed admirably and the singers were in great form. We spent a very pleasant evening.

Today is Sunday and pay day. This morning Bob and I went to early service and except for a rifle inspection and pay parade this afternoon we are free. I have a nice book – "Tom Sawyer" by Hall Caine – and a pipe, so I shall be alright. The room is warm and cosy and all I want to make the conditions ideal is an armchair and you.

I am coming home this week, exactly which day I cannot at present say, as the batch for last week were put back a day or two.

For a little while then, au revoir dearest.

With all my love. Yours, Ted

No. 94 **"Saturday" (postmarked Sunday 19 December 1915)**

I have reached France at last. After your Dad saw me off we went to Dover and then back to Folkestone for some unknown reason. We did not get on the boat until nearly 4 and sailed about 5. We spent the night here in a rest camp (in tents) and although it poured with rain from the time we left the quay until now, our tent was nice and dry. Many were very wet and the whole place was a quagmire. We had blankets and I had a splendid sleep from 10 o'clock until 8 this morning. Needless to say after our brief spell of paradise I dreamt of you. In fact I kept dosing (sic) in the train yesterday and several times I leant my head forwards to rest on yours which seemed still to be on my shoulder.

Dearest, I think you are so patient and brave. I know what that smile of yours cost you yesterday morning when we said Goodbye and I do appreciate it and love you all the more for it. Thanks so much for that effort. It is an effort to put on a brave and cheerful smile when the heart is nearly breaking.

I have taken the opportunity to just hurriedly pencil this note as I know youwill

Footnote to No. 94:
Charles Randall walked with Ted from Lewisham to Victoria Station to catch the 5 am leave train.

be waiting for one. Keep brave, darling and with that "au revoir". You know I love you.

Yours ever, Ted

P.S. Thank your Dad for coming to Victoria. It was good of him.

No. 95 **20 December 1915**

I expect you are still looking for a letter from me. I rejoined the battalion yesterday after a journey by train, motor lorry and transport waggon, spending one night at Lillers. The boys were coming out after a short spell in the line and we are now in a small village in reserve for a few days. I have been transferred to no. 6 platoon and had not time to write yesterday as I am for the present platoon sergeant. I am quite well and found the other fellows fit also. By the way Storch and Bob are in my platoon. They were pleased to know you sent your love to them. "Sonny" is acting CQMS.

We are celebrating Christmas day tomorrow and are to have special bill of fare. Roast pork, I think, but I will tell you all about that later. I hope for a letter from you this evening. You know what your letters are to me, don't you darling.

With all my love, Ted

No. 96 **21 December 1915**

Thanks for your letter of Friday. It came last night and I was so glad to get it. Today is so wet and the place is so muddy it is very depressing but we are as cheerful as possible under the circs. as today is our Christmas day. We are dining at seven this evening and that should liven things up a bit. I do hope your Christmas will not be too unhappy. Think of our "joy week" and be glad. I am glad to know that, although this beastly business has to go on, I am lucky enough to have the love of a woman whose love means more to me than anything and the thought of which buoys up my hopes that one day when blessed peace is again restored we can enjoy each other's love to the full.

My darling, how I miss the caress of your soft hands and the sight of your serious grey eyes which speak such volumes, but I know that your whole being is just waiting for me as I yearn with all the depth of my burning love to once more clasp you to me. Your loneliness, now that I have perforce left you, pains me but what can I do? I feel so helpless to comfort you. You have all my love.

I am so glad you are so pleased with the little watch. I hope it goes well.

It is kind of your Dad to think so much about me.

Now dearest, au revoir. Yours ever, Ted

No. 97 **22 December 1915**

We have another day of comparative leisure so I take the opportunity to write again to you. I may not be able to for a day or two, after today. Our Christmas evening was quite a success. Our menu was roast pork, potatoes, cauliflower, apple sauce, onions etc. followed by plum pudding and tinned fruit.

This morning there was a voluntary church service – communion and carols – in the recreation room. This room is a boon when in billets which are not private houses where one can be comfortable.

The enclosed is a copy of the snap I told you of and which I wanted to get. Don't you think it is a good one? A fellow who had a complete set gave it me when I told him I wanted to send it home. The other fellow in the foreground is the late Sergt. Dangerfield ("Delts") and it is a good photo of him. There is not much to write about.

I had a little parcel of cigarettes and chocolate from Mr and Mrs Thatcher. It was good of them as I did not know them very well.

Give my kindest regards to your Dad, Charlie, Edey and Grace.

Heaps of love. Yours, Ted

No. 98 **28 December 1915**

Thanks for your letters of 21st and 23rd. They reached me in the trenches yesterday morning. Yours of the 19th reached me on Christmas eve. We went into the trenches on Thursday morning and spent three days in the reserve trenches in slush to our knees. It rained practically the whole time and we were all wet through and muddy. On Christmas day we saw nothing of the trench festivities which the papers describe this morning. The artillery started before it was light and the enemy replied rather severely and the duel of shelling lasted all day. On the evening of Christmas day we moved up to the firing line for our turn of two days in. Boxing day was still wet and the trenches in places were waist deep in water. The part we were in was not so bad, but we got so wet wading through the communication trenches. Many fellows went sick through exposure, and yesterday I was sent to the Field Ambulance with "water-bite" or "trench feet". I had not a very bad attack but I have been sent back to a field hospital where I now am. My feet went all spongy and white with the continual soaking but are better today. I am having a day in bed today.

I expect to be back with the battalion in a few days so continue to write as usual so that I can get a lot when I do go back; Bob will save my letters for me. Storch had a nice Christmas box. He was sent on leave on Christmas day – straight from the trenches.

Thank Grace for the Christmas card and tell her Bob's chicken was the next size larger.

I believe Stan is sick somewhere but I have not seen him for about six days.

I expect I shall lose my parcels through being here but it cannot be helped, I suppose.

Was Mother pleased with the things you got? Christmas must have been a miserable affair for you my dear, but I hope you made the best of it. I thought all day about you and old Bob and I sat in the mud and had a good old "jaw" about things at home and tried to cheer each other up.

We also got some Christmas pudding, and a card like the enclosed was given to each man. It is a drawing by General Rawlinson.

Now, darling, I must close as it is getting near bed time. We have lights out early here. My feet burn a little but I think that is because they are now so hot, being wrapped in wool. Do not worry, It is nothing serious.

Good night my beloved. I think of you always.

You have all my love, Ted

No. 99 **30 December 1915**

There is not much to write about as I have not a letter of yours to reply to. I have now been sent to the Corps Convalescent Company for a short time. My address is as usual but with IV Corps Convalescent Coy. added. A letter may reach me if I am here long enough. I arrived today. The place we are in is a huge old convent – very picturesque – and I am in the sergeants' mess which I think will be very comfortable. My feet are better but still tender. I lost my boots and have been given new ones which does not improve matters much. I also lost my old overcoat – the one I have had all through. In fact I lost all my kit, so I have nothing except just the army equipment. It seems such a blank without your letters but I shall continue to write just the same and you know I shall remember you and know you are remembering and writing. Each time I feel my identity disc it quickens my memory of the happy time we had together while I was home. I hope you always wear the little watch and that it is going alright.

Did you get the little snapshot alright?

Kindest regards to your Dad and Charlie.

Au revoir, my darling. Yours ever, Ted

No. 100 **31 December 1915**

I cannot let New Year's Eve go without just writing a little. Of course I still have no letter from you but I believe I think of you all the more.

We are not so very far apart; are we?

I even dreamt of you last night. Why was that? I wonder if you were thinking very much of me, then.

I do so hope that this New Year which we are about to start upon will bring Peace and see the end of the awful carnage of war. I pray that before next December we shall be together again happy in each other's love, and therefore I wish you a Happy New Year. I know that if you are happy I shall be also.

Au revoir, my beloved. Ever yours, Ted

JANUARY 1916

New Year's Day saw the 20th. cleaning up in Sailly-La-Bourse after its front line activities over the Christmas period; they marched to fresh billets in Houchin on 2 January and the following day were inspected at Les Brébis by the Corps Commander (General Wilson), the Divisional Commander Major General Barter) and the Brigade Commander (Brigadier General Thwaites). The Church Square in Les Brébis was shelled three minutes after the battalion left to return to billets.

When the 47th. Division relieved the 18th. French Division at Loos on 4 January no overground accommodation remained in the village. The 20th. took over the "copse" section from the French 135th. Regiment, with 'A', 'C' and 'D' Companies in the front line with 'B' Coy. in support in the "Enclosure" and in the "Tranchée des Anglais". The 18th. London held their left flank and the French 135th. were on their right. On the Feast of the Epiphany (6 January) the opposing German infantry tried to make overtures from behind their barricades. There was some anxiety over suspected and rumoured mining operations but these fears proved groundless and no mine was blown. Three Germans surrendered to 'D' Company of the 20th. on 9 January.

The next day the 20th. left the forward trenches again to return to Maroc which was heavily shelled on 11 January and a further move was made to Noeux-les-Mines. After Church Parade on Sunday 16 January the Brigade Commander decorated Captain Waghorn and 2nd Lieutenant Muir with DCM ribbons before the battalion moved forward once more to relieve the 24th. London in the Maroc sector. A shell landed in the 'D' Coy. trench on 17 January killing Privates Wells and McClure[1] who were buried in Maroc. Three days later 'A', 'B' and 'C' Companies were holding the firing line on the double crassier south of Loos when Lance Corporal Wood was killed. The Battalion War Diary records the presence of the Brigadier in the front line trench at 06.00 hours on 21 January. The following morning at 02.00 hours a defensive mine was blown in the copse but it provoked little enemy reaction. Two days later the 15th. London (the Civil Service Rifles) relieved the 20th. who enjoyed a four day respite – including the Kaiser's Birthday (27 January) which was a "windy time" for front line troops – before returning to the right sub-section of the Loos sector on 28 January. That day lacrimatory shells fell on Maroc.

1 L/Cpl A. R. McClure was an Old Roan; his brother Douglas survived the war, rising from the ranks, and commanded the successor battalion to the 20th. in 1939–40.

No. 101 **2 January 1916**

Dearest,

I am still in the Convalescent home and going on well. I hope you are quite well. We have an easy time here and the rest should do some good. Today, being Sunday we had a Church service. It was quite a good one and being the first Sunday in the year I was glad I went.

For some reason or the other it made me long very much for home and you, especially so, when after the service we had prayers for "those at home". You can imagine the mixed feelings better than I could describe them.

There is very little to write about so I hope you will not find my letters too uninteresting.

You know that my Love grows stronger the longer we are parted and I know that you will never tire of my repetition of that fact. We spend our days in the sergeants' recreation room with magazines, draughts, cards etc, but having nothing in particular to do gives more opportunity for thought and I can assure you that you are hourly in my mind.

Au revoir, my darling.

With all my love. Yours ever, Ted

No. 102 **4 January 1916**

I am still here but am now quite fit again and shall rejoin the battalion tomorrow.

I am looking forward very keenly to getting some of your letters then and if the opportunity occurs I will write tomorrow evening in reply.

There is nothing more to tell you so "au revoir".

With all my love.

No. 103 [Maroc] **6 January 1916**

I reached here, a village behind that part of the line which our battalion is holding (a different part, by-the-way, to that which I left) yesterday evening and this evening I am going up to join the battalion. Storch is with me, returning from leave. We were glad to see each other. I hear Bob is in hospital and Stan is still, I believe.

I am still without any letters from you or home, but I am in great hope now of getting them in the morning.

There is nothing more, so au revoir, my darling.

With all my love. Yours, Ted

P.S. If fine, will write from the line as soon as possible.

No. 104 — 11 January 1916

We are now out of the trenches – more or less – and are in cellars of wrecked houses where we get some strafing occasionally.

I am in receipt of your letter of the 3rd but have not got any arrears yet. We are leaving here tomorrow night and I will write fuller then. The present circumstances are very unfavourable for writing owing to shortness of candles. We pass the time by holding choral society practices as we can sing in the dark.

For the present dearest, au revoir. You have all my love.

Yours ever, Ted

P.S. I met Will James the night I came up, at his Battalion stores. He is very fit. I hope to get a good job soon. I have have put in for it. Wish me luck.

More love, Ted

No. 105 — 14 January 1916

I received your letter of Tuesday last today, together with your Dad's and his photograph. It is a good one. You had quite a merry little party on the 1st apparently. I am glad as it afforded you a pleasant variation. I had a letter from Harry today.

I was also pleased to hear that you had a good time at Hampton. Jack and Wendon have every reason to thank the lucky Fate that sent them to India. I wish we could get a turn there. I was sorry I missed your Christmas parcel but the fellows who shared it said it was a real good one.

The cake they say was a "topper". Did you get a letter of mine which contained a little snapshot?

I like the large photos of myself a copy of which arrived in your letter that I acknowledged on a field card yesterday and all my pals out here think it is good.

You seemed, when you wrote that letter, to be rather "down". You must really cheer up, my dear, – things will not always be as they are. You have been brave right through and things do sometimes look rather hopeless but you must let hope buoy up your drooping spirits and look with me, forward to the time when "all will be fair". I often sing as much of that song of yours as I can remember and of course that brings all sorts of visions.

Thanks for distributing my photos. I heard from Mallett that he had got his. Would you mind getting some more p.c.s? Dad will pay you for them. I want one for Bob, Storch and "Sonny" sent out. We have heard from Bob.

There is not much in the way of news. We reached here, N.....les M......., for a few days the night before last. For the present then "au revoir" dearest.

You have all my love. Yours ever, Ted

P.S. Mallett is very pleased with the photograph. He paid a visit to the office the other day and had a chat with the boss. The boss said some nice things about me and I hope he will think the same when I get back.

No. 106 — Sunday 23 January 1916

You will be wondering why you have not had a letter lately – no opportunity. We are as you see in the line and you know what that means. We had two days in cellars, but spent the time sleeping.

Things are quieter this morning and it is a lovely day. So bright and crisp, with heavy frost at first but brilliant sunshine now. A day like this is refreshing. We had a lively night of bombardment. We exploded a mine not far from here in the early hours and that caused a little argument. We have also had some excitement in dodging the enemy's giant trench mortars. Charlie will remember them at Givenchy nine months ago.

I have now your letters from the 6th to the 18th and will attempt to reply to them all now.

I was much amused by your description of the charades at Harold's 'party'. A nice thing to make fun of a chap's suffering(?) isn't it?

Now about those waterproof socks you contemplated sending. Don't! Storch had some and they wore thro' the first time he wore them, owing to the boot sticking in the mud and causing friction when pulled out; besides that, they are not a success.

Thanks so much for your parcel. I was billeted with Storch when that and one from Mother came. We had such a jolly feed. The mincepies were absolutely A.1 and in fine condition too. It came on the evening before we moved up and what was not cleared off then – not much – we brought along with us. When next sending please send some pipe cleaners and "bachelor" buttons. I still have the woollen helmet as I stuck to my pack alright. I keenly await the arrival of your photograph. I am glad you have having one done and hope it will fit my pocket.

You are apparently having a busy time at the office, with so much overtime. Grace says you do a lot (with tongues). Which reminds me I must write her soon.

Glad you got the little snap. Did Charlie recognise the place?

Yes, I knew Fred Goosey had got a "home service" commission. He is unfit for service abroad. I was surprised to hear that Salmon was still at home. I knew about Crocker being wounded. We have had a letter from him. Was sorry to hear about Charlie Hammond. Please let me know if Charlie gets any more news of him. it looks as if Bob will be away a long time. We have heard from him. Sonny has gone to hospital now with some illness or the other. He looked very bad, poor old chap. I am now platoon sergeant of No. 8 platoon so when next writing you had better leave the platoon out of the address altogether.

Captain Cowie is in charge of the company now, but we all wish "Mac" Escombe would come back.

That programme you suggest in one of your letters would suit me admirably. It was a topping moonlight night last night and I thought of it then and had to blot it out of my mind. One cannot dwell too long on such thoughts without beginning to feel covetous and rebellious.

The weather generally while we have been here has improved although the trenches were a little wet when we came in.

You know, dearest, how I am always thinking of you and it makes me glad to know that you dream sometimes of me.

The night before last here in this dirty little dugout I dreamt I was somewhere peaceful with you. I do not know or care where it was, but I was divinely happy – and then woke up to do my tour of night patrol. Still I had just the memory of a dream to think over and I was still happy to know I had someone of whom I could dream like that.

There is not much more to write about, so once more, au revoir, my beloved.

With all my love. Yours, Ted

P.S. "Coram" is his stage name.

No. 107 **25 January 1916**

Thanks for your letter of 20th. We are now out of the trenches for a few days but are not far back. I have a fairly comfortable billet however and tonight we are arranging a dinner party which should be a success. I am still quite well and trust you are. We came here last night and were very glad to get a good sleep in blankets, as the last 24 hours in the line was spent in a sap out in front of the line and I had no sleep as the sentries, for some reason, got "wind up" and imagined Germans were creeping about only a few yards in front of us. It was a pitch black night so perhaps that accounted for it and they were tired.

We were allowed to light no fires but we managed to get some tea by boiling a mess tin in a little dugout with a tin of dubbin as fuel.

The job I put in for has been given to Sergeant Williams in 'A' Coy, so that's that, as Geo. Robey says. I have, however, sent my name in, in response to a request for nominations for the 1st Army Survey Company. I may be more lucky with that.

I say, next time you are doing fried fish and chips at cookery class, stick some on a post card and send some out here. I could find it a good home. You could send enough for the platoon I should think. It consists of 4 men, 2 stretcher bearers, 3 lance corporals, 1 corporal and myself – some platoon! My section used to be bigger.

There is not much to write about. You know all I would tell you. How I want you and just long to see you.

Au revoir, my darling. With all my love, Ted

No. 108 **27 January 1916**

Thanks for Sunday's letter. I am sorry you were so long without a letter but by now you have got one. You tell me of the cinema at Peckham, but you little think that we have a cinema here. It is a divisional affair and gets just packed. The admission is 2d and after the trenches it is refreshing to see a few films. The remarks from the audience are, however, quite the chief item of the show. Of course the place, an old school, is not very luxurious, nor do they serve dainty cups of tea.

I have received Grace's letter. I must answer it soon, but my correspondence is getting something abnormal. I can never seem to write all the letters I would.

We shall be moving up again tomorrow so I am afraid field cards will be the order for a little while.

I do wish with you that this was all over. One grows so sick of it all at times and then things seem to all look black but we must grin and bear it, I suppose. Things can't go on like this for ever. Oh I would give something to have another leave so that we could be together if only for a little while.

I just live now with one hope that of getting back to be with you and to enjoy your love.

Au revoir darling. You have all my love, Ted.

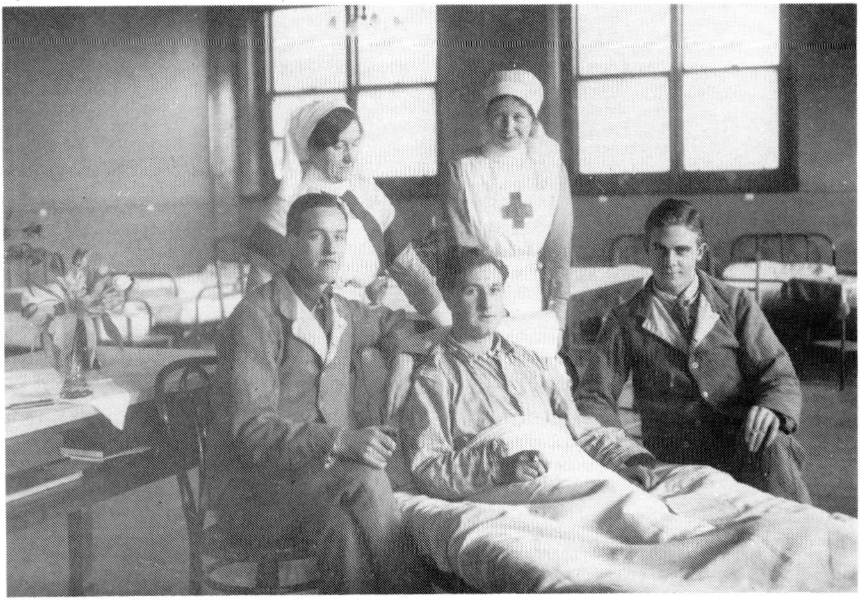

Stan Trafford (on left) in Hospital. ? Béthune, 1916.

FEBRUARY 1916

The winter weather was unusually wet and cold but the 20th. had another two weeks of trench duties before a break was expected. Artillery activity predominated while the infantry concentrated on survival.

On 3 February our artillery staged a demonstration bombardment of "Sniper's House" and "The Barricades" but a number of high explosive shells failed to explode and the exercise was repeated the following day. The 20th. was relieved by the 8th. London on the 5 February and moved out to Braquement where all troops were billeted by 03.00 hours the following morning. Later a working party of three officers and one hundred men reported at Fosse 2 to rendezvous with the Sappers but the latter failed to arrive and after waiting an hour and a half in intense cold the party returned. The Battalion Bathing Parade on 7 February was welcomed by all.

During the evening of 8 February the Company Commanders reconnoitred the Maroc section of the line which the battalion took over the next evening from the 23rd. London. 'A' and 'B' Companies were in the front line with 'C' in a new support line and 'D' in reserve. Two quiet days followed during which the Brigade Commander visited the front line. On 12 February in a burst of enemy activity, G Sap was blown in by a 90lb. trench mortar bomb killing three bombers of 'D' Coy., and another man was killed in J Sap. Artillery retaliation followed and the dead were buried in Maroc. Two days later the Germans exploded a mine near "Snipers House" and at 04.00 hours the next morning, bombers of the 19th. London made a counter attack while the 20th. "stood to" to provide any covering fire necessary. During this action a man in 'C' Coy. was blinded by a rifle grenade in J Sap.

The anticipated "rest" for the 20th. came on 15 February when the 2nd. King's Royal Rifles took over the Maroc Section, the battalion reaching Braquement without casualties by 03.00 hours on the 16th. There was a gale and rain and heavy kit was carried in lorries from Les Brébis. Later in the day the 20th. marched to Noeux-les-Mines, entrained to Lillers and them marched to billets in Cauchy à la Tour. Notwithstanding the atrocious weather the troops' morale was high. The Brigade Commander visited the battalion the following day during "cleaning up" activity and the C.O. inspected each Company on 18 February.

A new draft of reinforcements was inspected by the Brigadier on the morning of 19 February; the rest of the day was occupied in clothing issues and the usual fatigues. During the day Lieutenant Colonel Hubback departed to lecture officers of the 3rd. Army on the Battle of Loos, leaving Major Dolphin temporarily in command of the 20th. Sunday 20 February was marked by a Church Parade in the canteen; a small fatigue party worked at the flying ground at Auchel. On Monday morning the Battalion Transport paraded for inspection by the Brigade Commander at Ferfay crossroads. A training schedule was announced for the rest of the month involving daily working hours of 09.00–12.30: 14.00–16.00: and 17.00–18.00, followed by evening cinema entertainments. But the very next day, heavy snow caused the abandonment of the training programme only part way through the morning; the Chaplain held an impromptu meeting in the school after tea.

Despite further snowfalls, training continued for the next four days. Colonel Hubback returned to the battalion and Major Dolphin departed on leave on 23 February; officers attended a lecture on artillery cooperation at Rimbert on 24 February. All leave was cancelled for the 1st. Army on 25 February (possibly on account of the snow?). The new draft passed musketry tests "fairly well" the next day.

A partial thaw set in on Sunday 27 February; the customary Church Parade was held in the late morning. The battalion rehearsed Parade Ceremonial on Monday morning; in the afternoon HQ staff and bombers lost a football match against the 19th. London, and there was a concert in the recreation room in the evening.

The weather relented and remained fine all day on 29 February, when a Brigade route march was held. An ammunition reserve was established at battalion HQ comprising twenty boxes of small arms ammunition, eighty-four boxes of Mills bombs and two boxes of rifle grenades.

No. 109 — 4 February 1916

Dearest,

Thanks so much for your letters, the last I received was yours of the 30th which arrived the night before last. I expect another tonight. I cannot quite remember which was the last I acknowledged in my last letter, but I am sure I have missed none as I look out too keenly for them for that. We have just done four days in the first line and are now living in cellars of wrecked houses, like rats or moles, and emerge only at night time.

We were in a fairly hot part but sustained, in this company, no casualties, thanks to underground dugouts where we kept ourselves concealed during the day (except for a minimum number of sentries) and where the shells did little more than shake us.

We are constantly shelled during the day here but our cellar is a fairly strong one and although we have had several shells through the upper part of the place, of which there is not much left, we only get showers of dust and clouds of smoke down here and our candle extinguished. We have been in semi-darkness owing to lack of candles but have now contrived a very passable lamp with a tin, a piece of flannel and anti-frostbite grease – a mixture of tallow with which we are issued. This is our third day here and tomorrow night we go further back, I think. At night we go on working parties into various parts of the trenches where damage has been caused and repairs are necessary.

Thanks very much for the parcel. I can tell you that the whole of it was appreciated. It came the first day we were here and was enjoyed in comparative comfort (we have chairs and a table down here).

You ask me in one of your letters if I ever plan things for us. Of course I do. It is one of my chief topics of thought when I think of you which is very frequently. I have made up my mind that when all this is over and I return that we will be married and have our own little home as soon as I can possibly, by diligent work, increase my income enough to make the scheme workable. I mean to make you happy to repay you and make up to you for the months of anxiety you have endured so stoically.

And now we come to another delightful little episode. You cannot tell how pleased I was to get your photograph. I like it immensely and so do a few pals I have shewn it to. It is the best I have seen of you and I shall, naturally, treasure it.

Sorry, if I muddled a bit with mine, but when out here with so much to think of you know it is easy to do a thing like that. Thanks for sending the extra three.

Bob has written me to the effect that he is now on a P.B. (permanent base) job. Sonny is back at a base hospital with jaundice.

I don't know what the "Survey Coy" is and I have heard no more of that, but the machinery of the army is slow.

Glad you had a nice fine day at Maidenhead. I suppose you had a few "recollections". I had when I heard you were going.

I am very surprised to hear about Nellie but I wish her the best of luck.

Now dear, I have had quite a nice chat with you (I wish I had really) so I will close with yet another assurance of my love and a loving "au revoir".

Yours ever, Ted

P.S. Enclosed is one of the men from this Coy. wounded at Loos – 25 September.

P.S.S. Am short of "baccy".

Footnote to No. 109:
Pat's cousin Nellie was to marry an American.

No. 110 — 6 February 1916

Thanks for your letter of the 3rd enclosing yours of 31st December. I could not make it out as I started to read that one first.

We are now out of the line and in billets. We reached here at about 1am this morning and I had to parade again at 8am with a party to go working on a new road in course of construction about 3 miles from here. I got back at about 2pm. It was hard to get up as I am in a comfortable billet with another sergeant, where we share a double bed. He is a nice fellow and an acquaintance of Mallett.

We are here I think for four days.

The air raid was, as you say, terrible but I do hope with you that they will keep away from your neighbourhood.

I forgot to tell you of our slight experience of "weeping" shells. The Germans sent a few over when we were going up to the line last time. Not sufficient to be really serious but enough to be very uncomfortable. The shells emit a gas which at first has a very pleasant smell but which as it becomes more pronounced is decidedly sickly and makes one's nose smart and eyes water. We were all weeping freely and exhorting each other to "Cheer up" and "Oh! dry those tears".

There is nothing more to tell except that I am tired and must soon go to bed.

Good night, my darling. You have all my love.

Yours ever, Ted

Footnote to No. 110:
On the night of 31 January 1916, 6 or 7 hostile airships made widespread raids on the Eastern, North Eastern and Midland Counties of England.

No. 111 — 8 February 1916

I expected another letter today but have been disappointed so far, but I take the opportunity to write you as we shall be off up the line again tomorrow, for the last time before our month's rest, we all hope. You will not mind posting the enclosed will you? I have, altogether, written seven letters this evening. Quite an effort what? Yet I still could write more. We had a delicious bath today at a local mine. These bath days are one of our anticipated pleasures. Two days after a bath one begins to look for the next. There seems very little to write about when I have not a letter to reply to but I must write just a little bit to let you know I have not forgotten you. I rarely do that I assure you. Thoughts and memories of you are the patches of sweet among the bitter and Oh! how I look forward to a long and undisturbed enjoyment of our mutual loves. I want you more and more.

Good night dearest. Yours ever, Ted

No. 112 — 18 February 1916

You will be wondering why I have failed to write before this but we have been on the move back again and I have had no opportunity. We arrived here yesterday by the same method as when we came back for our last rest. We are not at the same place but at the next village, less than a mile distant. I have just been, with Storch, to our old billet, where the four of us were so comfortable. The good lady was so pleased to see us and the little boys went nearly mad with excitement. I left them one of my photos to their great pleasure. We had the worst weather in the trenches this last time that I have ever known. It blew "great guns" and we had rain and snow with it which lashed and stung one's face like little whips, but that is over for a while now I hope. To give you an idea of the force of the wind, we saw a convoy of transport waggons which had been blown clean off the road, some of them with the top part blown right off the wheels. Your parcel arrived while we were in the line and very welcome it was too. The "potted" meat was delicious and saved me and the lance corporal with whom I shared a dugout from the monotony, for at least a day, of our bully beef ration. Thanks very much. It was nice to get your Christmas letters, I think I must have all that I missed, by now. Thanks also for the second photograph. I cannot decide which of the two I like best. They are both fine I think. You had an enjoyable weekend with Elsie Phillips apparently.

I was very sorry to hear of Gordon Tolhurst's death. It must be a great blow to his Mother. I think that in a case like his the dear ones left behind are more to be sympathised with than the one who meets his untimely but nevertheless glorious end. I expect you feel it too for he was, I know, a great friend of yours.

"Sonny" is still at a convalescent camp somewhere and I think he will soon be back with us. Bob, I hear has a job at Rouen – lucky beggar. Storch is quite well but in another platoon. I have a comfortable billet. I have a bed which I share with another sergeant in one place and our mess is a few doors away and very comfortable. It is here that I spend any spare time I may have.

I am afraid you are not very happy at home. Are you dear? Never mind, take consolation in the fact that one day – not far distant I hope – we shall have our own little home where we shall both be happy.

Now, dearest, good night. With all my love, Ted

No. 113 — 21 February 1916

Thanks for your letters of the 16th and 17th. We are still "out" for our rest, but I think it will be a rather strenuous one as the authorities seem to have a somewhat extensive programme of drill, manoeuvres etc.

The lot of a platoon sergeant is a busy one commencing at 6.30 – reveille – when one has to go round and rake the chaps out and acquaint them with the day's orders. Then come the parades; physical drill first then ordinary military drill until one o'clock. More parades at 2 until 4 and tonight we had an NCOs lecture at 5. All the "spare" time is spent with "indents" and "returns" and then one has to wait up until perhaps ten o'clock for the next day's orders.

Things are not too bad though. I have a "batman" or orderly to clean my rifle and see to equipment and run messages etc. and the mess is very comfortable. It is very cold today and freezing hard. It looks like snow. We have had a little today.

I have not forgotten the date and I remember how eager I was to get out of hospital a year ago. I had not seen you then for over five weeks and that seemed an age. What a time it seems now since I saw you last! I am beginning to look forward to my next leave, it ought not to be <u>very</u> far off, about three months at most and who knows but what this beastly war may be over by then, or nearly so. I do not think it will last many more months, if all goes well as it should do and then what unthinkable joy shall be ours after so much "wasted" as you choose to call it – I prefer apparently wasted or seemingly wasted – time.

Now, my beloved, Good night and God bless you. I think of you and love you all the time.

Yours, Ted

Footnote to No. 113:
In February 1915 Ted had been confined for several weeks in Camberwell Fever Hospital (the 1st London General Hospital) suffering from Scarlet Fever.

No. 114 — 24 February 1916

Thanks for your letter of 20th. We have had some very hard weather. The day before yesterday we had a very heavy fall of snow but despite that we paraded as usual and tramped about in it. In the afternoon we paraded and had a glorious snowball fight. Yesterday we had a route march in a perfect blizzard and today we have been doing outpost duty – a rather cold job. Thank goodness we have a comfortable place to spend our evenings and a room to sleep in. It would be terrible in the trenches now as it looks as if we were going to get some more of it. Everywhere is very picturesque and really some of the scenes about here are positively lovely but it is not the sort of scenery one would like to spend many hours amongst.

I should very much like to know what happened to cause Will Pike to revert so drastically. I suppose you have no idea and I do not know his address.

There is very little to write about but you know all I would say. How I want just you and how fortunate I consider myself to have a girlie who loves and cares so much about me. You have all my love darling. How I just live for the time when we shall be together and, as you say in one of your dear letters, have our own little home. How happy we two could be together.

Goodnight, my beloved. Yours, Ted

P.S.If not asking too much I should like a pair of large-sized cape, heavy kid or leather gloves with warm lining. My trench gloves are worn out.

No. 115 **27 February 1916**

Thanks for your letter of the 22nd. I do hope that you were not too worried at not hearing from me for what seemed such a long time. We are still in our good billets although the weather is still cold and the snow stays about. There was however a slight thaw today which has now ceased and the freezing continues.

There is very little to write about. Our days are spent on parade. Yesterday we had a slight variation in the shape of a birthday supper. Corporal Dunphy in my platoon, a very fine chap too, celebrated his 21st by inviting all the old men, who came out with the battalion, in Nos. 7 and 8 platoons to a supper. He got a fine spread including champagne and we spent a very enjoyable evening. We had songs afterwards but no piano which was rather a drawback.

The chap I sleep with is Sergt. Hicks. He is quite a nice fellow and is an old school chum of Mallett. He is a good singer and is always in demand at concerts etc. which we arrange. He and Hammond whom you met one day outside the Library, were great pals. He is as tall as I, too.

We had a church parade today: of course not in a Church as they are all Roman Catholic, but in a barn. Still it was quite a good service.

No more, at present dear. With all my love. Ever yours, Ted

P.S. Please don't forget the gloves. I want them badly.

A Puzzle for Paderewski
"It's a pity Alf ain't 'ere, Bert; 'e can play the piana wonderful"
See Letter No. 115
From *Fragments from France* – Bruce Bairnsfather.

MARCH 1916

Bad weather predominated for the first half of March making unpleasant conditions for the continuous training programme, which had to be abandoned for the day on 1 March, though that evening officers of the 20th. attended a lecture by Major Batty at Rimbert on tactical reconnaissance.

Captain Andrews RAMC left the battalion on 2 March, posted to Rouen, and was replaced by Lieutenant Stableford RAMC; the same day 'D' Coy. won the final of the Brigade football competition and the officers heard another lecture – this time by the Brigadier – on the French Army manoeuvres which he had attended.

On 4 March the 20th. marched twelve miles through snowstorms to new billets – and not very good ones – in Enguinegatte. Four days of field training in dreadful weather followed; newly arrived mobile cookers were given a thorough testing as hot meals were served each day in the field. On 8 March came the news of Colonel Hubback's promotion to Brigadier General and appointment to command the 2nd. Infantry Brigade; he addressed the battalion and bid farewell to all ranks. The officers held a dinner to celebrate the anniversary (actually one day late) of the sailing to France. The only officers remaining from the original battalion were present – Colonel Hubback, Major Dolphin, Captains Williams and Clout and Lieutenants Lovibond and Taylor.

The 9 and 10 March were occupied in moving on foot, in raw cold weather to Calonne Ricouart with an overnight stop in Bailleul-les-Pernes. During the weekend of 11/12 March, a draft of fifteen men plus 2nd Lieutenant Maxwell arrived from Vaudricourt and a Church Parade was held in the village school on Sunday morning.

But the battalion was returning to the front; Monday was a beautiful day as the troops marched via Divion, Houdain and Fresnicourt to Servins for two nights in "comfortable" huts. (Clearly the Adjutant in writing the War Diary had not seen the rats which abounded in the huts!)

The move into the line started during the afternoon of 15 March but heavy enemy shelling forced a two hour halt in the ruins of Carency before the 20th. finally took over 'A' sector of the Carency Section shortly before midnight from the 1st. Worcestershire Regiment. The 20th. had the 19th. London on their left and the 4th. Lincolnshire Regiment on their right; they took over very shallow trenches in poor condition, which required 48 hours of intense hard labour to put them right, the work being hampered by enemy shell and trench mortar fire, though less sniping than might have been expected. During six days in the front line there was considerable enemy activity – mainly from artillery and trench mortars. Sergeant Cole of 'C' Coy. did particularly well one night; from a shell hole in no man's land, with a supply of bombs, he was able to keep down sniper fire against the working parties repairing the trenches. Sergeant Hewett was killed on 20 March – a loss greatly felt after his exceptionally good work.

The Battalion was relieved by the 8th. London at 23.00 hours on 21 March and marched out to Estrée Cauchy, packs being carried by lorry from Villers-au-Bois where hot tea was served. Billets were reached by 04.00 hours; cleaning, re-kitting and training occupied the next two days. More snow fell on 24 March causing the cancellation of the Brigadier's inspection of Battalion Transport. A working party of eight officers and four hundred men assisting the Royal Engineers returned soaked through in the evening. Major Carr (24th. London) arrived as acting C.O. The following day, the 20th. mustering 13 officers and 247 other ranks, marched to Olhain to take part in a Brigade Ceremonial Parade and inspection by General Wilson, Commander of IV Corps. Later in the day a fatigue party of 100 men worked for the R.E.s while there was also a bathing parade at Fresnicourt. Sunday 26 March saw the customary Church Parade and more bathing.

On the Monday morning, the 20th. marched to Gouy-Servins and occupied the chateau vacated by the 23rd. London. The rest of the month was occupied in providing working and carrying parties to support the troops in the line. A reinforcement of 2 officers and 24 men joined the battalion on 28 March and on that evening the Chaplain gave a cinema entertainment in the chateau. A demonstration with a captured German "Flammenwerfer" was given to the 47th. Division on 29 March. The Brigade and Divisional Commanders jointly inspected the 20th. London's billets on the last day of the month.

No. 116 **1 March 1916**

Dearest,

Thank you for your letter of 25th and parcel of the 24th. It was a nice little parcel. I was in need of Handkerchiefs badly.

We are still in "the little place of rest" and on Sunday we went to a town near here and had the enclosed photographs taken. The Frenchman who took them is little more than an amateur, but he has got them done quickly. My only regret is that "Sonny" is not in it. He came back last night, quite unexpectedly and I tell you he got some reception. I was glad to see him. The other two photographs of two of my pals were of course taken in England and I want you to look after them for me.

I am glad you had a pleasant evening at Anderson's. Alec would be pleased to be home I guess, especially as Annie is coming up to town.

I do not think I should be much better off if I had taken a commission in another infantry battalion. Do you? Especially when one remembers that my office pay ceases if I take a commission or at least, so I think. In addition to that, look at some of the commissioned "boys" you can see in the streets. I think I am alright now as "circs." are.

It makes no difference really how one does one's bit or in which uniform. Neither does it make any difference to our love for each other. Does it, dear? I just want you all the time.

Goodnight beloved. You have all my love. Yours, Ted

P.S. Please post enclosed card, with names "printed" on back, to R. T. Mallett, Esq., 27 Nightingale place, Woolwich.

No. 117 — 3 March 1916

Thanks so much for your letter of 29th February and also many thanks for the fine pair of gloves you sent. They are just what I wanted. My old gloves are good enough for trench wear, but they are torn with barbed wire etc. and worn too badly for ordinary wear. When in the line I can keep them in my pack.

Glad you went out with Lily and had a little change. You certainly need all the diversion you can get, I think. It relieves the anxiety, which I know you have for me; but just at present we are running very small risks. We certainly did have a Bosche aeroplane over here a few days back, but the bombs it dropped did no damage in our immediate neighbourhood.

We are moving from here to another place tomorrow, but more of that anon.

That is all for the present, except that I love you and want you all the time.

With all my love, Ted

No. 118 — [Enguinegatte] — 5 March 1916

Thanks for your letter of the 2nd which arrived this afternoon. It came very quickly as I see by the postmark that it was not posted until the 3rd. We are now some twelve miles from where I wrote from last. It was a little joke I think on the part of the authorities to decree that we should move to another area for training. So accordingly we played our little part in the game by marching here with everything we possess (and other things beside) packed all over us, on roads like quagmires, in a perfect blizzard that would have done credit to an arctic expedition, yesterday. We were wetted through and then to crown all we came into this hole of a place – a very tiny place with scarcely room to billet a battalion of ants; let along men – and were put into barns without the slightest chance of getting anything dried.

Our officer who at present is our late Sergt Burt and who by the way is still "Niffy" when his pals speak of him, found a billet a little better for the sergeants. I am with Sergts Hicks and Gardiner in a little damp room of the "Curé's" house. It is a tiny chamber without a fire or furniture and with a tiled floor. However we soon "foraged" for some clean straw to sleep on and have made it as comfortable as possible under the circumstances. The Curé is very nice but not too hospitable.

Today, as we have already had two Sundays something like ordinary Sundays since being back, we had an all day field exercise having our "dinner" out – cooked en route by the field cookers – and tramping all day over saturated ploughed fields. It rained and snowed at intervals just to keep our spirits up. Needless to say we were tired when we got back and we spent part of this evening, as we did last, looking for a place to get a good feed but were disappointed. The village does not boast a butcher's shop and all we could get was a meal of fried eggs and potatoes in a farm house.

We have no sergeants' mess here and "Sonny" is in another billet as he is acting Coy. Sergt Major. Storch is now a full corporal in another platoon so I do not see much of him. He somehow does not seem the same old Storch he used to be when "we four" all grubbed along together on our last "rest".

I think that those lobster cutlets would just "appeal to" me now.

I do not think Bob will get home, except on leave, as he seems to have a permanent job now. Could you get his present address? I have not heard from him for some time.

Have American letters been censored all the time or is it quite a new thing? I think all letters from abroad should be censored. Fancy Nellie getting married so soon! As you say they are not wasting much time. Is the fellow an American? I am afraid I don't think a lot of Americans in general. I hope and expect he is a nice chap though. When you write offer her my congratulations and thank her for remembrances please.

I wonder why Charlie went away in such a hurry. I expect you know by now. It was a shame to rush him off so quickly, but such are army methods. It seems ridiculous for Alec to go back so soon. Doesn't it?

I seem to have a cold coming on but it may be better by tomorrow.

I am so lucky to have someone who loves me as you do and whom I can think of so tenderly. it makes my lot with which I would otherwise get so "fed up", bearable when I think of what "we two" will be to each other one day. Dearest, your love gives me strength to "play the man". I only wish I could make myself more worthy of it. I can't see why you love me as you do, and yet I love you back with all my might.

Darling, I want you so much.

Good night. With all my love. Yours ever, Ted

P.S. Monday 6 March. Post is not collected until midday so I thought I would add a little. There has been a heavy fall of snow during the night and everywhere is white again. The cold seems a little worse, but is nothing serious and I have been to see the doctor who has excused me duty for today. I shall have a rest in the blankets today. Cheer Ho!

No. 119 — 11 March 1916

Thanks for your letter of the 5th. You will wonder why I have not acknowledged it before but we have been "on trek" again. We moved off the day before yesterday from where I was billeted with the curé and yesterday we came on to here, a village not far from where we were when I sent you those photographs, staying the night at a small village where I got quite a decent billet. We should have liked to have had a little celebration dinner on this night as it was the anniversary of our sailing, but the place did not boast a butcher's shop so we just broached a bottle or two of champagne. We reached here yesterday afternoon very tired and found a butcher's shop and got a jolly good meal. We turned in early. I have a nice bed on the floor and the four sergeants, Hicks, Gardiner, Thomas and myself, live together. We shall be having a slack time today, with a game of Rugby this afternoon, but I will describe that later.

Please excuse more for the present.

With heaps of love. Yours, Ted

No. 120 — 12 March 1916

Many thanks for your letter of the 7th which arrived last night. I am glad you liked the photographs. So you think my "chic" cap makes me look like a German? I am very fond of that old cap. It is the one I wore when on leave but with the flaps for the ears cut off. Corporal "Pat" is one of the original men who came out with us as a private. He is now a lance sergeant. He is not a "bosom" pal but an awfully solid sort of chap and one whom I like very much.

Please thank Grace for her little compliment. I have not told Hicks what she said about him. It might make him conceited. I hope you will see "Sonny" one day when we get back again to the "piping times of peace".

I can quite imagine that Bob's letter was funny. I got one too which he had "painted" with his typewriter. He said he was doing all his correspondence with it that afternoon. I wondered how far into the night that afternoon extended.

It was a lovely day today – just the sort of day for a nice walk with you. Wouldn't the opportunity be a fine thing? We had more snow last week but it has all gone now. You seem to still be startled in the night hours by the "Zepp" scares.

It was just like the "impetuous Bob" to write to tell Elsie his address and then leave it out.

It was rather strange that you should see Len Shaw and sister at the Concert at the parish Hall. The Stephanian Dramatic Society is in connection with St Stephen's Church.

We had a very strenuous Rugger match yesterday between this Coy and a team representing the rest of the battalion. We just won by 6 pts to 5. The ground was a bit slushy and the fellows who played in ordinary trousers got into a fearful state. I had a pair of shorts – old khaki bags cut down and a singlet I got from the local "Selfridge's", while for stockings I wore two pairs of socks, one with the feet cut out for the legs.

We had our usual Church parade this morning, but Sundays are like ordinary days out here except just for the morning and this afternoon I am playing in a Soccer match with a team of Frenchmen from this neighbourhood. It should be rather humorous.

There is nothing more of interest to write about. You know well how much I want you.

With all my love. Yours, Ted

Footnote to No. 120:
On 5 March 1916 a Zeppelin raid over eight Eastern Counties of England left 13 killed and 33 injured on the ground.

No. 121 [Servins] **14 March 1916**

Since writing you last we have made another move, this time forward towards the line. We came here yesterday. It was a long way and the weather was quite hot as it is again today – quite like spring and were it not for the continuous roar of the guns it would be hard to believe that there is a war on at all. We are in a fresh part altogether and away from the mining districts. The country around here is the best we have struck but all the roads are very hilly. The people are not at all hospitable and we are glad we are not billeted upon them. Instead we live in huts in as fine a mud flat as you could find anywhere. In addition the huts swarm with rats and it is only the fact that we sleep on raised bunks which prevents them running over us at nights.

We expect to be going up the line tomorrow but do not worry, girlie dear, I will write at least a field card as often as possible.

There is a lot to do today in the way of final outfitting after our period of rest and writing here is not a very easy job, there is little convenience and a lot of noise. Now dear once more au revoir. I think constantly of you and you know that you have all my love.

Yours ever, Ted

P.S. Thanks for "Punch".

No. 122 — 18 March 1916

Thanks for your letter of the 13th and for the "K.M." and the delightful parcel. I do not think you could have packed into so small a space a more dainty and at the same time useful little collection. The sausages fried up with the bacon made an excellent breakfast, while the lobster cutlets fried up formed a tasty part of today's midday meal. We still hold the fruit and cream and cakes in reserve, for a later indulgence.

We are as you may guess in the trenches, but we have been lucky so far in having fine weather. This afternoon however we are getting a little rain which we do not want.

The trenches are still very muddy, the result of the snowfall and we have an awful job to keep the sides up owing to the wet state of the ground. On our way up here we passed through some ruined villages, the like of which I have never seen before and we have seen a few. These places are absolutely levelled, a fact which testifies to the fierceness of previous fighting. I have a fairly comfortable dugout although the water drips through the earth quite a lot. It was I think originally built and occupied by the Germans and since then has been successively used by the French, Germans, French and now by the English.

I wondered why I did not get my usual Sunday letter from you but the Monday one came nice and quickly to make up for it.

I am so glad you had some company for the weekend. Elsie Phillips is such a lively person and you two should have enjoyed a merry time together, apparently you did.

You also had a nice little tea with Elsie on Friday last.

The night before last as I slept in short snatches I continually dreamt that I was somewhere with you, I can't say where or when but we were so happy, as happy as I hope we shall be one day when all this is over.

I just want you so. You know that don't you?

With all my love. Au revoir sweetheart. Yours, Ted

No. 123 — 21 March 1916

I was delighted to receive your two letters of the 15th and 17th which arrived one last night and one the night before. It is lovely to get an extra one when one doesn't exactly expect one, although I am always on the lookout for one from you. We are, I hope, being relieved tonight so I shall be unable to send this off until tomorrow. My platoon is in support now and has been for the past two days. We do not live in a trench here but in dugouts on the reverse slope of a hill, the firing line being on the top. The scene from here would be a fine one but for the landscape being marred by several, what would be pretty, little villages in hopeless ruins. Even the woods which are included in the extensive view, are nothing more than a collection of charred poles. The poles being tree trunks which still stand although shorn of branches and scorched by continuous shell fire.

It must have been a pleasant change to get a few hours off last Tuesday without the usual troublesome application and an even greater pleasure to attend your friend's wedding. I rather like the idea of the quiet little ceremony you describe and you wished it were our wedding, did you, girlie dear?

I wish also it had been; but it will be one day. "One day" sounds very vague and far away. Doesn't it dear? Yet it will come and I do hope it will not be too long. I should be so happy making you happy as you deserve to be to repay you for your long, loving anxiety.

I am afraid Elsie Smith has been misinformed about leave as one of my corporals went yesterday. It has been stopped for a time and has just restarted, although all the men who came out, and are still with the battalion have not been yet. There are not very many, however.

I still look back on our "joy week" and shall continue to do so with pleasure until we enjoy a more joyful one next time.

So you have signed for your holiday. Dare we hope that by then we shall be able to spend a holiday together? It seems too good to think about.

It seems ages since I even had a Saturday's half holiday, although it was a very great pleasure to get a game of rugger last week. I got a bath after it but not like the hot ones I got at home.

It was with a pail of cold water in the yard.

You ask me what I think about the end of the War being in sight. There is every reason for optimism, that is all I can say, although I don't think there is harm in mentioning that we captured a prisoner who is reported to have said that the Germans here are very dispirited and half starved and that it is only the Prussians who keep them in the trenches and do the strafing. How true the report is I cannot say. There is nothing more at present. I have written quite a long letter for the line. Haven't I?

I want you just as much as ever.

With all my love. Yours, Ted

I hope you can read it – the light (a candle) is poor and I have nothing stiff to write on. Cheer Ho!

[Estrée Cauchy] **22 March 1916**

Thanks for yours of the 19th. it is such a nice letter and I was so pleased to get it. We arrived here, a village quite a good way back at about 4 a.m. this morning. We were all very tired and turned in at once. I did not wake up until 2 this afternoon and have just breakfasted at 4.30. Post is just going.

No. 124 **25 March 1916**

Thanks so much for your letter of 21st. We are still in the village I wrote from last but the fairly decent weather we have had lately seems to have ceased again; yesterday there was a thick layer of snow when we awoke and it continued to snow nearly all day. In spite of this we were out on an all day "working party", digging trenches for use in case of emergency some miles behind the line. It was a very cold job, some distance from here too and when we got back at night I felt in no mood for writing. Today has been a busy or at least a very full one and it is too late now for this to go off before tomorrow. We had more snow in the night but this morning is quite sunny and thawing. The Corps Commander, General Rawlinson, inspected the whole brigade this morning at a place some miles from here and we got back at about two, had some grub and then paraded for baths at a place quite near where the inspection took place. The bath was quite welcome as we had not had one for some weeks. We do not get such good baths now that we have left the mines but a bath of any sort is usually welcome. We did not get back to billets until about six so you see we have been fully occupied. I shall finish this and post it tomorrow now.

Thanks for "Punch" which has just arrived.

Goodnight, then, beloved. I hope you will sleep as soundly as I know I shall after I have lain for a little while after the light is out and thought of you and home. I may even be lucky enough to dream of you.

Sunday 26 March 1916

It is raining this morning and nearly all signs of the snow have gone. We are having a church parade this morning and a day's rest after that. Quite a change!

I would like to be spending a Sunday like we used to spend, but we shall one day. I just want you more and more. You have all my love.

Au revoir, dearest. Yours ever, Ted

P.S. I am quite well. How are you? Kindest regards to your Dad.

No. 125 [Gouy-Servins] **29 March 1916**

Your letter of Friday last has just arrived. All the letters seem to have been delayed and I was beginning to wonder if yours had gone astray. I had not heard from you for several days and they did seem to drag without your usual dear little notes. We have made another move and are now in an old Chateau. It has been a very fine old place but is now considerably the worse for wear. I and my platoon are in a loft over what were probably the stables. It is cold and the lighting is not good but we make it as comfortable as possible.

From here we go up to the line each night as working or carrying parties and return again in the early morning. We sleep until about mid-day and then it is nearly time to be getting ready for the evening again. We have had more cold weather. It blew and "sleeted" a perfect blizzard last night and we came in with a suit of ice armour on. It is trying to snow now but I hope it will clear up before we start off. There seems very little to write about and there are official threats to stop the issue of green envelopes as some have been abusing their use.

I do wish I could express all I would tell you in a letter.

How I just long to take you in my arms and say all that would be necessary to make you happy and that would make me happy.

Au revoir, my dearest. With all my love, Ted

No. 126 — 31 March 1916

I was very pleased to receive your letter of Sunday, yesterday. We are still "carrying on" as when I wrote you last.

I was out last night and did not get up until dinner time (1p.m.) today. I stayed in bed – a piece of wire netting on a wooden frame like a light hammock, with two blankets – and read a book which I have had lent to me. It was quite a nice little story. You may have read it "The Blue Lagoon" by H de Vere Stacpoole. Have you? I also read a few days ago at odd times "The Girl of the Limberlost" by Gene Stratton Porter. That was a fairly well written story but very light reading and not very interesting. A book especially an interesting one in a cheap and easily portable form is usually welcome and can usually be "swapped" for another when finished with. One can often read when one cannot write.

I am sorry to hear that your Dad has been queer. I sometimes think he is too energetic for his age. Do you think he tries to do or rather does too much? I hope he is better now. Please give him my kindest regards.

Did you experience much of the "great blizzard"? It is quite fine here today and it was a grand starlit night last night. Since I have been out here I have seen some glorious nights, sunsets and dawns. I quite enjoyed being out last night. We were carrying stores up to the firing line. The road we used consisted of trench boards (like bath mats, only larger) set along what had been a road but now resembles a stream owing to a small river being chocked with debris and overflowing. Except for that and the ruins it would have been hard to realize that a War was on. For some reason or the other there was a big lull in activities.

I have heard that "HMS Pinafore" is a pleasing operetta but I have never seen it performed. I must ask Hicks to give me some selections.

How is Grace? Give her my love when you see her please. If you can spare her the tiniest little bit.

The news in the papers seems to be a little more cheerful lately and I do so hope that my surmise that the end is in sight is right.

Now, darling, au revoir, with all my love. Yours ever, Ted

APRIL 1916

The month opened with an inspection of the 20th. London Transport by the Brigadier on the Fresnicourt – Gouy–Servins road. The next morning the Battalion marched back towards the line, resting in Villers-au-Bois, before relieving the 23rd. London that evening in section A1 of the Carency Section. The 20th. had the 19th. London on their left and the 5th. Leinsters on their right; the trenches were in very poor condition, holding a great amount of mud and water, but the battalion stayed for seven nights. A lot of hard work was done to deepen and strengthen the trenches and there were regular exchanges of artillery and trench mortar fire. A German aeroplane was shot down behind the Leinsters' line on 3 April and an enemy mine blown in front of that unit on the 7th.

The 8th. London relieved the 20th. during the evening of 8 April and the battalion moved out via Carency to Estrée Cauchy in the course of the night. Packs were carried by lorry; hot soup was available en route and the men were in good heart. Sunday 9 April was a quiet rest day; after a voluntary Church Service the Brigade Commander visited Battalion HQ and addressed all ranks on the good work already done in the line and on the need for continuing effort while in support and reserve. The next four days were spent in physical work and training; new trenches were dug in front of Gouy–Servins and Carency despite two wet days, and there was bayonet fighting, bombing and musketry practice. Carrying parties took new mortars up to Carency. The bathing facilities at Fresnicourt were used again on 11 April.

On 13 April the 20th. marched to Bouvigny arriving before midday and taking over hutted accommodation from the 24th. London. In the afternoon officers reconnoitred the Lorette trenches in readiness to take them over the following evening from the 23rd. London. The relief was duly effected though it was a wet night and the rain persisted the next day. Battalion HQ was established in Ablain St. Nazaire. Late in the evening of 15 April a heavy bombardment opened up on the 23rd. Divisional front to the left (north) of the 20th. Around 22.00 hours enemy aircraft engines were heard overhead; considerable air activity followed the next day, in bright clear weather. At noon there was heavy fighting on the front to the right of the 20th. whose observers felt that the British artillery had been slow to respond to rocket signals for help. At 16.00 hours on 17 April twenty-eight shells fell on the road between Ablain and Servins, giving rise to a fear that this supply route was visible to enemy observers on the "pimple" – a mound at the northern end of Vimy Ridge. Three companies of the 20th. worked all day on the construction of a new support line. From 21.30 hours the ration dump at Ablain St. Nazaire was shelled every five minutes with salvos of high explosive and shrapnel. Our gunners retaliated against the German batteries at 22.00 hours. The next day at 19.00 hours a mine was seen to be blown ahead of the 46th. Divisional front line. 19 April was again a wet day and our artillery took the initiative but provoked no response. However, at 22.45 hours, the enemy opened heavy fire from the right of the "pimple" and sent up many red and green rockets. Was this a ruse to make our troops think that a mine had been blown and to expose themselves in a rush to seize a non-existent crater?

The 20th. was relieved by the 8th. London during the evening of the 20 April, with 'A' and 'B' finding cover in Carency; battalion HQ, the bombers and 'C' Coy. at Villers-au-Bois, and 'D' Coy. temporarily attached to the 18th. London. Day and night working parties in the support area became the regular duties of the battalion. At Church Parade on 23 April, a beautiful day, the band of the XIX Hussars accompanied the hymns. A case of measles was diagnosed the next day, necessitating the temporary isolation of 'C' Coy. and the bombers. Shells fell on Carency during the day, the enemy trying to silence a French battery.

The 20th. handed over to the 6th. London on 25 April and moved back to Verdrel to be comfortably billeted in huts; but 'D' Coy. remained behind attached to the 18th. London holding "Ersatz" trench on the right defensive flank of the divisional front. They rejoined the battalion two days later.

The rest of the month was spent in routine activities – cleaning up, re-equipping, bathing, inspecting and etc. The guns in the Carency section were heard constantly but the peace of Verdrel was shattered only once – at 11.00 hours on 28 April when three shells fell in the Bois de Verdrel.

A field Church Parade in full marching order was held on Sunday 30 April, after which ceremonial drill was practised and the battalion inspected by the Commanding Officer. A second voluntary Church Service was held in the evening. And so the 20th. prepared for the most eventful month since its arrival in France thirteen months earlier.

No. 127 **4 April 1916**

Dearest,

I was very pleased to get your letter of the 31st ulto. this morning and very many thanks for the parcel which arrived on the 1st. The saccharine is especially useful now we are in the line again. We have had a spell of glorious weather but today is very dull misty and cold. Yesterday was quite like summer and the day before, Sunday, was also hot. We marched about half way here at midday and then waited until dark before continuing. It was lucky we came by a different route this time as the road we used last time was shelled heavily. Our company is in reserve in the dugouts I described before and yesterday some of our chaps were bathing in the flooded shell holes in the valley; some of these holes, made by monster shells, are as large as ponds. We spend our days in sleeping, eating, reading etc. and our nights or at least, a good part of them, on working parties. This is much easier than the usual trench routine. In fact it is quite a rest although the front line is only some 200 yds away.

These few wild violets I picked on the side of our hill. There was evidently a small wood there and it was also evident that the spot was the scene of as terrible an encounter as was ever fought. All the trees are cut down or shattered and even the craters formed by shells were each fortified and used as miniature trenches. Despite all this the beautiful little violet peeps out just here and there as if to remind one that, although hard to find, the bright spots still appear. With me, my little violets, which I am glad are more numerous than the enclosed, are the sweet thoughts of your love through all.

I do hope your Dad is better. I am sorry to hear that he has been so queer. Give him my kindest regards.

No more at present, dear.

With all my love. Yours ever, Ted

No. 128 — 6 April 1916

I was delighted to receive your letter last night, written on Sunday. It would have been lovely, as you say in one place, to have had that or any day together just we two. How happy we could be. It would not make the least difference whether it were fine or not. We should be satisfied to be together. Shouldn't we?

Sonny, lucky beggar, is leaving here tomorrow and should be home on Saturday. You may see him. He will certainly be seeing Elsie Smith and he may invite you with her out to tea. Do go, there's a good girl. I want you to meet him and some of my other "pals" when that is possible.

Yes, we heard about the Zepp being brought down in the Thames and were of course frightfully bucked. Two days ago we saw a "Fokker" brought down behind our lines.

I am glad your Dad is getting better again. Five days enforced idleness must have seemed a long time to him and he must have been pretty queer to have stayed in bed for that period. Give him a "Cheer Ho!" from me please.

We are still on the hillside and altho' the weather is not wet it is scarcely "fine".

Footnote to No. 128:
The Zeppelin L.15 was shot down in the Thames on 31 March while attempting to approach London.

It is quite cold today and the nights are of an inky blackness. I have rarely known it to be so dark as it has been these last few nights.

It is nearly time to have tea now and there is not much in the way of news to tell, so I will close down.

You have all my love, my "Patie" (sic), au revoir.

Yours ever, Ted

No. 129 — 8 April 1916

Your letter of the 4th reached me last night and needless to say it gave me the usual pleasure. You certainly seem to be going at top pressure at the office, but Cheer Ho! "C'est la guerre" as the French say with a shrug of the shoulders when things go amiss. It was some time ago that you last went and met Lily wasn't it? You don't tell me much about yourself my dear. I usually say just that I am still fit or otherwise, but you never mention yourself or at least you rarely say how you are. I trust you are quite well.

So pleased to hear that your Dad is well again. Tell him so please. Thanks for the promise of a book. I think with you that Gene S. Porter's books are quite pretty stories and well written, but that is about all, but I can read and enjoy most books now after having a rest from reading to any extent for quite a long time. We are still on the "hill" I described but are making another move tonight, so this letter will not go off until tomorrow.

"Sonny" went off yesterday and from where we are I watched the communication trench he went by to see if any shells went that way but no, he got away quite safely and should be almost home by now.

I had a rest from labour last night but I stayed up until nearly midnight waiting for the post and I was rewarded for my vigil with your letter and one from Elsie. It was a fine but cold night last night with a clear sky and a thin crescent moon. It was lighter and much better on that account. The night before when I was in charge of the carrying parties was a beast. Raining all the time, the only rain we have had this trip, which made everywhere as slippery as ice and as black as pitch. It was a good thing that I had a decent dugout to get a good sleep in. Mine is like a little grotto dug out of solid chalk and is quite picturesque. I call it the Robber's cave. Not on account of the human occupants, myself and a private who acts as orderly and platoon runner, but because of the rodent occupants, swarms of mice, and visitors in the shape of rats. It's a wonder that these rats don't chuck us out and have the place and our rations to themselves. They have almost enough cheek for that. We had quite an exciting rat hunt last evening but they are so artful and have so many holes that we only killed one.

That is all, for the present. You know that I think almost continually of you and that my Love is all yours.

Au revoir, my beloved. Yours, Ted

Sunday 9 April 1916

P.S. Arrived here in the early hours of the morning. O.K.

No. 130 — 12 April 1916

Thanks for your letter of the 7th. I do not feel as if I can write much today. Things are going on just as usual – the same monotonous round. I am quite well.

I am pleased that you have made some arrangement for Easter. You and Elsie Phillips should have quite a good time away in the "little country place" together. At any rate it will make a very pleasant change for you. I should very much like to be able to be there with you, but let us hope it will not be so very long before such an opportunity is ours.

I expect "Sonny" is beginning to count his days now. I remember how I did and how the blessed time would just fly. Storch is going home today to take up a commission as is also Sergeant Dunphy, known to you as "Corporal Pat". Sergeant Thomas, who was in that group we had taken, went home yesterday with time expired. He has completed nine years in the "terriers" and been out here with us for 13 months, so I think he has done his "bit". What?

You mention in one of your letters that you will probably get me a book or two. Thanks! but let it only be one at a time please.

Now girlie, that is all at present. I just long for you.

With all my love. Yours ever, Ted

No. 131 — 16 April 1916

I am afraid you will be wondering what has happened to me and that I am awfully mean not to have written lately. Well I have been shunted from pillar to post ever since I wrote last. On the night of the date I wrote last we were out on a working party until 3 a.m. Then next morning we paraded at 8 a.m. (not much sleep) and marched away to a village some distance off and behind another part of the line. Next day we moved up to the trenches – not the front line but some support trenches whose chief feature seemed "mud". (We have had quite a lot of rain recently.) The next day I was detailed to attend a "course". These "courses" are classes for a week at the Corps School of Instruction at a kind of advanced base right back from the line. My "course" is one of physical exercise. To continue the history, that night I went back to our Quartermaster's Stores and stayed until next morning (today) when I had to report at Brigade H.Q. (two villages away) and from there I came here by motor bus. We are in tents here and I believe we shall be kept very busy, but more of that anon.

For the present all that worries me is the fact that for six long days I shall get no letter from you. But it is better here than "up the line" at any rate.

I will write, however, and I hope you will, just the same so that I shall have several when I go back.

Au revoir, then, once again my dear. With all my love. Yours, Ted.

No. 132 **18 April 1916**

I am still in the camp from which I wrote on Sunday and the two days I have been here have both been wet, so it has not been very enjoyable. In our class we do exercises all day long. It is rather tiring but the idea is to make us into physical training instructors to our battalions.

There is very little to write about as I cannot answer your letters yet, not until I get back. The last I had from you was dated the 11th. I also got your Dad's letter. Please thank him for it. I got Grace's letter too and I will reply to her when I get time. I do miss your letters. It seems such a long time to go without them – six or seven days at least.

That's all for the present, dear. You have all my love. Au revoir, Ted

No. 133 **Good Friday 1916 (21 April)**

I am still without a letter from you and I wonder what you have been doing today. With us, it being Good Friday has made no difference except that we paraded a quarter of an hour earlier for a short Church service. It was a fine day for a change today but was unfortunately too good to last and now, this evening, the rain is just pouring down again. This week under canvas might have been quite enjoyable but for the wet. The field in which the camp is situated is one huge quagmire now. I doubt if I shall be able to get this letter off from here as today's post has already gone and tomorrow afternoon before letters are collected I shall be on my way back to the battalion. I am feeling very fit and I hope you are quite well. I shall not be able, I find, to get this off until tomorrow evening when I get back, so I will finish it then.

Good night, my beloved, I hope my tent will keep the wet out tonight as it looks like being a very wet night.

Saturday evening

It is still raining and has been all day. We paraded at two this afternoon and had to wait two hours in the downpour for the 'buses. At last when we were all thoroughly wet they came and here I am at the battalion stores where I shall spend the night and rejoin the battalion in cellars and dugouts in a ruined village up near the line.

Just before I left I got a few letters, one of them from you written last Sunday. It would certainly have been like an old time Sunday had Stan and I been at home to complete the party. I don't quite like the fish shop idea and my particular role requires more sinews than intellect. The farm is better if someone knew anything about farming. I am glad you had a little outing with Elsie Smith. I have only seen her that once but I think she is awfully nice and of course I have heard a good deal of her.

Sonny is as you suppose, on his way back, but he went sick at Boulogne and is now there in hospital. Thanks so much for the little white violets. I like them, because you are so fond of them. Dearest, I want you so much. I am just living now for our next "joy week". Au revoir, my darling.

With all my love. Yours, Ted

No. 134 [Verdrel] 25 April 1916

I am in such a muddle with my correspondence, I scarcely know which letters I have replied to and which not. Some of my letters were sent on to me and reached the school after I was back here and have followed me here. I received today yours of the 18th and yesterday yours of Good Friday. So you did go away after all. I am so glad and I hope you had a jolly nice time.

The parcel you sent me was treated like all parcels which arrive for men who are away from the battalion – namely, "scoffed" by his pals, as parcels cannot be redirected and they certainly cannot be carried about. I did not mind that as at different times I have helped in "scoffing" other chaps' stuff.

The man who used to act as my orderly saved the socks for me and I was very glad of them.

We came farther back today and we are now in huts built on a fine site on top of a hill with lovely country all round. There are some beautiful woods near by and they look splendid with their fresh spring leaves and bright flowers. I was only in the cellars for two nights and yesterday went up to the front line with a working party. Our job was to get some of the water caused by the recent rains out of the trenches and to clear up the mud. In places they were a foot deep with slush.

It was a fine day yesterday and is even better now. It was far too hot to march, really, this afternoon.

Has the little "affair" at your office been cleared up yet?

What sort of a place is Cranleigh? I expect by the time you get this I shall have heard all about it.

Leave does not seem to get any nearer. For the present all leave is stopped. I had a letter from Bob a day or two ago with one of his photographs. I think it is a jolly good one of him.

Now my darling, Good night. I would just love to kiss you Goodnight and hold you tight for just a little while. I want you all the time and I constantly think of you.

With all my love. Yours ever, Ted.

No. 135 **28 April 1916**

Thanks so much for your letter of Monday last, which arrived yesterday and for yours of the 14th which reached me today after a travel round the country to find me.

We are still in the huts I spoke of and the weather is perfect. We had a working party last night but are not going again tonight. I have just been for a stroll through the wood. It was gloriously peaceful and the rumble of the guns not so very far distant was the only disturbing element, but one gets so used to them that at a distance they are scarcely noticeable. The birds are not in the least disturbed by them. The nightingale is heard nightly while cuckoos, thrushes and all kinds of birds can be heard all day.

There is a very heavy bombardment on now and as it gets darker the flashes can be vividly seen. I hope nothing serious is happening to cause us to be rushed up.

I am so glad you had such a pleasant Easter. I certainly should have liked to have enjoyed some of those walks with you. At any rate my leave will certainly be before the summer is ended and I hope we shall yet enjoy such a walk, together, as you describe. The house you stayed at sounds very attractive and picturesque.

Now darling, I am off to sleep now, in a wooden arrangement like an egg box, but in which I sleep very soundly. I hope I shall dream of you. I certainly shall think of you as I always do before I drop off to sleep.

Goodnight. Will all my love. Yours ever, Ted

Officers and NCO's of 'B' Company 20th. London Regiment. 21 July 1916.
(Ted Trafford – centre, back)

MAY 1916 VIMY RIDGE

May Day was celebrated by an inspection of the 20th. by Major General Barter, G.O.C. 47th. Division, at Olhain. The battalion was played past by the band of the 17th. London and the General commented favourably on the turn-out. A fatigue party of 200 men worked in the evening. The next day the battalion returned to the support area taking over the chateau at Gouy-Servins from the 24th. London; it rained on the march, but the next day was fine and companies were left to themselves to clean up. Lieutenant Needham and the Chaplain arranged a concert in the theatre in the evening. A few evenings later the troops were entertained by a concert given by the band of the Brigade Field Ambulance (the 5th. London Field Ambulance from Greenwich and Deptford). For a few days the 20th. were out of the action, though well aware of the activity in the Carency section. Three officers, including the C.O., and thirteen other ranks left on home leave; there were demonstrations of sandbagging and wiring, and lectures on Lewis and Vickers machine guns. A Church Parade was held in the R.E. lines on Sunday 7 May, before the 20th. moved up to Villers-au-Bois. During the afternoon the Company Commanders reconnoitred 'A' section of the Carency section, which the battalion took over in the evening, relieving the 21st. London. Their immediate neighbours in the line were the 17th. London on their left and the 11th. North Lancashire Regiment on their right. In the fortnight since they were last in the line, the 20th. found that four mine craters had appeared between the opposing front lines (named Kennedy, Gunner, Love and Mumbert); our bombers held the nearer lips of all except Gunner and were able to deny the enemy possession of the craters. The 20th. had seven Lewis guns in the front trench, and four Vickers guns, four Stokes mortars and six medium mortars in the second line. The trenches had all been badly shaken by artillery fire.

There was considerable enemy artillery and mortar activity during the evening of 9 May to which our troops retaliated. Lieutenant E. G. Burt (formerly Sgt. "Niffy" Burt – an Old Dunstonian) was severely wounded, and the only other officer in 'B' Coy. had already become a casualty. Ted Trafford, as Acting C.S.M., was then the senior rank among the survivors of 'B' Company and he took control under the command of Captain Guy Williams of 'A' Company. A working party of 100 men from the 19th. London was given the task of coming up in the evening to assist in consolidating the crater positions, but they were seriously hampered by enemy fire and the exercise had to be repeated for four consecutive evenings. On 10 May there was artillery and mortar fire during most of the day and at 19.00 hours a bombing attack on Irish crater (is this an alternative name for Kennedy?) combined with a very heavy barrage on Zouave Valley. One observer states that this was the first use by the German Artillery of the "box barrage"; it was effective in isolating the 20th. troops in the front line and severing all communication for several hours. Light activity continued through 11 May (when Lieutenant Stutterford was wounded) and then at 05.00 hours on 12 May, the enemy blew a "decoy" mine in front of the Gobrun trench, but this diversion passed quietly as there was no crater to be contested. A comparatively quiet day gave way to a peaceful evening and night enabling appreciable reconstruction and consolidation of craters and front line to be carried out. On Saturday 13 May there was heavy artillery fire on both sides after the enemy had blown yet another mine on the right of the 47th. Divisional front at 19.15 hours. Owing to rain, the trenches were reduced to a very muddy state. The following day was quiet and in the evening the 20th. were relieved by the 21st London. The battalion was clear of the trenches by 23.30 hours, moved to Villers-au-Bois where tea was waiting and lorries to carry packs, then marched on to Estrée Cauchy. Colonel Matthews had arrived during the day to assume command of the battalion. Five days of rest and relaxation followed, during which Colonel Matthews inspected all companies; there was a little drill, bathing at Fresnicourt, another evening concert at the Brigade Field Ambulance and a cricket match versus the R.A.M.C. which was won by the 20th. Beautiful summer weather set in.

Late in the evening of 20 May the battalion was back in the line in the now familiar 'A' section Carency Section, with the 17th. London on their left and the 8th. London on their right, and with the 18th. (London Irish) in support. Sunday 21 May was the beginning of five days of intense fighting for the 20th., who suffered severe casualties. At 03.30 hours the enemy started a heavy bombardment which continued all day, becoming particularly intense at about 15.30 hours. At 19.40 the enemy infantry attacked Love and Mumbert craters and the 20th's front line positions and all along the front for a considerable distance to the right, i.e., along Vimy Ridge. An entry was made into the front line trench held by 'A' and 'B' Companies, but the enemy was ejected by a counter attack led by Captain Taylor. The battalion on the right of the 20th. had been forced back into their reserve lines, placing the survivors of 'A' and 'B' Coys. in a salient which could not be held; so after a stubborn resistance they retired to the support line which was double blocked – as was the old communication trench to the front line. This established a defensive flank linking the craters with the new front line now taken up by the battalion on the right of the 20th. The German artillery throughout, had shown remarkable precision; the 20th's front and support lines had been flattened and the barrage did not lift until the enemy infantry were half way across no-man's land. (The front lines were only some 60 yards apart.) Captains Taylor and Young were both killed by shell-fire in the course of this action.

On 22 May, the battalion bombers, led by 2nd Lieutenant Weston, drove the enemy from Love and Mumbert craters which had been occupied in the initial stages of the assault the previous evening. The 20th. planned to retake their old front line as well but this was impracticable while the enemy still held what had been the front and support lines of the neighbouring battalion on the right. The rest of the day passed quietly apart from some annoyance from enemy trench mortars and our own artillery unfortunately shelling our own lines causing eleven casualties including 2nd Lieutenant Lomas DCM, killed.

The losses sustained by the 20th. made it impossible to continue to hold the front line unaided; at about 21.00 hours the 21st. London moved up and took over the right half of what had been the 20th. front, i.e., the Love and Mumbert craters and the defensive right flank. The 20th. closed to their left, and reinforced by about 100 rifles from the 1st. London, held the length from Gobrun to Arnau (two communication trenches); one company of the 18th. London came up in centre support and another was kept in reserve. A counter attack by the 21st. London and troops on their right was considered for soon after midnight but was eventually postponed.

During 23 May, the 20th. front line between Tanchot and Coburg was completely blown in by a heavy artillery bombardment. The attack postponed from the previous night went in at 20.25 hours after 75 minutes of intense artillery preparation. The 21st. London retook the old front line but had to retire again after an hour as the battalion to their right had been unable to advance. But the 21st London did succeed in consolidating the trench junction between Gobrun and the old front line thus securing an alternative route to the craters. The front trench between Tanchot and Gobrun was blown in but the 20th. held the position from shell holes until retired to the support line early the next morning. During this action Captain Guy Williams, commanding 'A' Company, was severely wounded in the head by shrapnel. He was subsequently awarded the M.C. and bar for his exploits during this week in front of Vimy Ridge.

The 21st. London were relieved by the 23rd. at 08.00 on 24 May and artillery fire became less intense. The 20th. continued to hold the sector from Coburg to Arnau in front, support and reserve lines.

There was moderate shelling during 25 May but in the evening the 2nd. South Staffordshire Regiment arrived to relieve the 20th.; the hand-over was completed by 02.00 hours on 26 May and the remnants of the 20th. moved out to huts in Camblain l'Abbé. At roll-call, 'A' Coy. mustered 17 men in all, led by their CSM; 'B' Coy. had fared little better. Later in the day they moved on to rejoin the remainder of 141 Brigade in Estrée Cauchy and thence to fresh billets in Bours which were reached by nightfall. The next day was spent in cleaning up and then at Church Parade on Sunday 28 May, the C.O. congratulated all ranks on the good work done in the trenches. On the Monday came another short move – this time to Pernes – where routine fatigues and training, in the reserve area, were to be the order of the day for two weeks.

No. 136 **2 May 1916**

Dearest,

You will, I know, be looking out for this letter. It is longer than it should be since I wrote last, but I have been very busy.

For the last few days I have been acting as Coy S.M. the real chap being queer.

The weather now has improved steadily and we are having quite a spell of summer weather. Unfortunately we have left the place with the woods and are now at the village where we billet in a chateau which I have described before.

Sonny is still away from us. I do not know what is the matter with him.

I am glad Mother is better. I don't like to hear of any of my people being ill, while I am out here.

We were inspected by the General yesterday. It was a hot day and today has been just as hot and the heat was just killing when we marched here.

There is heaps I would say but I do not feel in the mood at all to write. I have felt like this for some days. It is quite an effort to bring myself to write at all. I have let my correspondents all except you and home go completely. I must when I get a chance clear up all my arrears.

You know that I think of you always and I want you more and more. The chance of seeing you seems very remote although I suppose leave must be getting nearer but it keeps being stopped altogether every now and again.

I am quite well and I trust you are. I have traced your book and I like it immensely. The one handed to me as being the one in your parcel is "The Way on an Eagle". That was the one you sent wasn't it? At any rate it's a fine tale.

That's all for the present, so with heaps of love.

Yours ever, Ted

No. 137 **5 May 1916**

I had your letter of the 30th and also your delightful parcel. Thanks very much for both.

We are having some really hot weather but I dread to think of a march in it. I am off duty today and not feeling quite up to the mark as a result of inoculation which I had yesterday. I hope the indisposition will work off before tomorrow as I have to attend at Brigade HQ tomorrow to demonstrate my ability to fulfil the staff job as physical drill instructor for which my name had been sent in by the battalion. Do you think that has anything to do with your dream concerning my transfer to the RAMC? I know you will wish me good luck in my venture. If I get the job I shall probably have a rest for a time from the line.

Thanks for going round and doing what you did for Mother while she was ill.

That reference of yours in a previous letter to the "river" haunts me this weather. I hope to have just one day when I get my longed for leave. We will be so happy in each other's love, won't we dear? We would be I think where-ever we were if we were only together.

I am longing to see you and just to give you one long kiss and a huge hug to make up for the long wait.

Good night! my sweetheart. With all my love.

Yours ever, Ted

No. 138 **11 May 1916**

I should have written you on Sunday last. I know how you will miss the letters, but do not think I have forgotten you. I am <u>sure</u> that not a day has passed since I have been out here without thoughts of you even for a little while.

I was sent on guard on Sunday evening when I had intended to write letters and was not relieved until Monday afternoon when I came straight on up here. This time we are in the front line, our lucky period of "reserve" being over, and in this part of the line things are getting very hot, with mines, trench mortars and almost continuous bombardments. It is a little quieter just at present this afternoon but each evening we have a rare old "strafe". On Tuesday evening we had the worst and another of the original "clique" went. This time it was "Niffey". I have told you about him before; he was Sergt. Burt but was made an officer. He got a nasty shrapnel wound in the back. I think, now, that I am the last of the 'set' who used to have such good times together. Sonny being still away from us.

I am still quite well and I trust that you are. The weather today is dry but it looks as if we shall get some rain tonight. Yesterday was fine but the day before it rained all day and night. This bit of trench is not very comfy, and we have no dugouts. I have just a little shelter where by curling up very small I can get a cramped sleep, if possible.

There is nothing more in the way of news except that my motto is still "Cheer Ho!".

I hope there will be a letter from you tonight. The last one I got was on Tuesday, dated the 5th.

I think very much of you when I am doing my nightly patrol and wonder whether all is well with you. Oh, my darling, I would just like to see you to see for myself. I would quickly kiss away your anxiety and comfort you and myself too, in one loving embrace.

Au revoir, sweetheart. With all my love, Yours, Ted

No. 139 **12 May 1916**

I hope this reaches you on Monday as it conveys your birthday present from me – My Love.

Fancy you being twenty two! You are getting quite grown up.

I am quite well. Au revoir, darling.

Yours, Ted

P.S. Thanks for Sunday's letter. It reached me at 1.30 a.m. today.

Footnote to No. 139:
15 May 1916 was actually Pat's 25th birthday. A little innocent deception, I think!

No. 140 **15 May 1916**

Thanks so much for your letters of the 10th and 12th. I received them both today. One when we arrived here at about 3 a.m. this morning and the other this afternoon. We had another soaking wet day on Saturday and altogether we were very pleased when our relief arrived on Sunday night and when we made our weary way here. We had not had a very pleasant time "up the line" and were indeed grateful to get a good long sleep today. You ask if we ever have little suppers now. Yes, we do sometimes, but they are not like those of olden days when we first came out. We had a concert too about a fortnight ago. I can't make out how I forgot to describe it. I usually jump at anything like that as a subject of a "newsy" letter.

I am glad to hear that old Bob has got home at last. I suppose you have seen him, by now. Do not envy Elsie Smith too much. This is Bob's first leave. Think how they both must have waited and waited.

Fancy Storch recognising her in Cannon Street amongst a crowd of people after having seen a photograph some months previously. He is a 'cute' chap.

You made a surprisingly good pun when speaking of the Bush boys in India by saying they are in Lucknow. I said they were all along.

I have never read, as far as I can remember, any of Gertrude Page's books but I will give you an opinion after I have read the one now on its way. The parcel should turn up tomorrow.

How was it you were staying with Elsie and Will on Friday night? Was it just for a little change or was Will out or something? I expect they don't much like the idea of Will being called up. Well, we shouldn't should we if we had settled down in a nice little place like they have.

I sincerely hope that you and Dad are quite well. I am as fit as can be and I am glad to know that Mother is better again.

Now, my darling, I must soon be turning in. I still feel tired although I have only been up since mid-day.

I shall as usual "think myself to sleep" in the short time that elapses between lying down and going off. My thoughts will be of you and how happy I want to make you.

Good-night, sweetheart. With all my Love, Ted

P.S. This won't be posted until tomorrow.

P.S.S. I forgot to answer your question about inoculation. I suppose that after so many months the effect wears off and the dose has to be repeated.

No. 141 — 18 May 1916

Thanks for your letter of the 15th to hand today and also for the parcel. The little coconut cakes are really topping and the shortbread is nice and in good condition. The lemonade is welcome this hot weather. The fruit and cream will also be very seasonable. We had a concert last night in one of the huts of the Field Hospital here. It was a great success and this afternoon was quite like old times. A team from this battalion played the R.A.M.C. a cricket match. They being more or less established in one place they have all the accessories and although we had not practised or played at all for so long, we beat them. Bob Cheesman was in great form, especially with his bowling. The pitch was not all that could be desired but we enjoyed the change very much. We are moving again tomorrow and expect to be in the line again in a day or two.

Charlie was a good boy to take you out to supper.

I am sorry to hear that he is still unwell.

I hope you had a nice time with Bob and Elsie. Yesterday afternoon I got permission to go and see "Niffey". He is still in hospital not more than five miles from here as he cannot yet be moved. He expects to be sent to England in a few days. He was very bad when first admitted there – in fact I think they had not much hope of his recovery, but I am pleased to say he is now very much better and was delighted to see me.

There is nothing more in the way of news.

You know well what I would tell you. How I just want you. This weather conjures up all sorts of thoughts about the river, alfresco teas, summer evenings etc. etc. How out of place the horrors of War are now, when nature is so beautiful. Still we must endure for a little longer. Be brave, my darling, don't get too discontented. Rest assured of my love.

Yours ever, Ted

No. 142 **30 May 1916**

It is some time since I wrote but that is not to be wondered at. We have been in a bit of a scrap. No doubt you have heard of it and I do hope you have not worried too much. We are now out and back for a much needed rest. Last Sunday week was the worst time I have had out here. The air was almost thick with shells, at times. We were relieved early on Friday morning and have been on the move since. I am now at the town where I was on the course [Pernes]. I wrote all there is to write about the place when I was here before. To get back again to Friday morning. We staggered out to some huts a distance of some five miles where we slept. It was our first proper sleep since we went into the line.

While here just before reaching our hut, I met Will Pike so he has come through alright. Sergt. Hicks was wounded on that Sunday and since then I have been acting Company Sergeant Major. We moved again after a sleep this time, a distance of about sixteen miles and yesterday we came on here. I am afraid a good many of our letters have gone astray, but I seem to have got all yours alright.

Sonny has come back today. We are glad to see him. He is well and looks very fit. I am quite well too. How are you? I got the K.M. today. Yes! that is Fred Wills, so he has a commission now. I have heard from Bob since his leave.

I have a good billet here and a bed to sleep in. Fancy Will joining the London Scottish! I expect Elsie will miss him. I wish he had joined some artillery or cavalry. Infantry is no good for him.

You are unkind to say that the cricket team should have lost because I played and you are all wrong too. I did play, so there! I shall have to write to Grace soon. She did send me a card and I think I still have it somewhere in my pack.

Now darling, once more au revoir. I am lucky to still be here and able to write to you, so please be thankful with me. I do so want to make you happy. I want to just take you in my arms.

With all my Love. Yours ever, Ted

JUNE 1916

Early June found the 47th. Division resting in the area between Bruay, Pernes and Diéval. The 20th. were at Pernes and provided daily working parties for the Divisional Battle School in Bruay and for the Fourth Corps Trench Warfare School. Firing parties visited the rifle range: physical training classes for officers and men were held; a riding class for officers; and a battalion transport competition. There was a voluntary service in the Church Army hut during the evening on 4 June; the Corps Commander lectured to all officers on the 6th; and Major Battye addressed the whole battalion on the 8th in the cinema hall. 141 Brigade held a ceremonial parade on 7 June in the course of a tour by the Lord Mayor of London to the London Territorial Division. Good bathing facilities were available to the Battalion during this period at the brewery at Pernes. The last day of this "rest" is described simply as "wet" in the Battalion War Diary.

In pouring rain on 11 June the 20th. moved back towards the line. By train from Pernes to Barlin and then marching to Verdrel to be billeted in huts. The parade state this day was 23 officers and 395 Other Ranks; six officers had remained at the Corps School in Pernes. The following day the 20th. relieved the 2nd. East Lancashire Regiment in the brigade reserve area, moving off by half companies at two minute intervals and marching to Fosse 10 at Sains-en-Gohelle. 'A' and 'B' Companies remained at Fosse 10 and 'C' and 'D' went on to Bully-Grenay. It had been a showery day but at its end the billets were good. Working parties of about 200 men were occupied each evening in carrying supplies forward to the support trenches. Captain Goodwin and 51 men arrived from base on 13 June to reinforce the battalion.

On 17 June the 20th. was relieved of these duties by the 22nd London, and the detached companies in Bully-Grenay rejoined the remainder of the battalion at Fosse 10. It was a beautiful day and at noon ten German aeroplanes came over the British support zone creating a deal of anti-aircraft artillery and aeroplane activity. There was further German air reconnaissance the following day after a midday Church Parade attended by about 80 all ranks. The Commanding Officer inspected the Battalion by companies outside their billets on Monday morning 19 June and later in the day, the Divisional Commander awarded decorations at the Bomb School at Fosse 10.

The 20th. returned to the trenches on 21 June, relieving the 23rd. London in 'A' sub-section, Angres sector; three companies were in the front line with one platoon of each in close support; one company was held in reserve. The 17th. London held the left half of the brigade front with the 18th. in support and the 19th. in reserve. Heavy rain on 23 June flooded the trenches and reduced them to a bad state not helped by some German artillery, trench mortar and rifle grenade fire. But night working parties were able to bring up gas cylinders and smoke bombs in preparation for a projected raid on the enemy lines. Such raids were part of the planned diversionary activity before the Somme offensive due to commence on 1 July.

The 18th. (London Irish) relieved the 20th. during the afternoon of 25 June, the latter moving into support positions – two companies in "Mechanics", one company at Cap du Pont and one company in Forest Alley with Battalion HQ in Bully-Grenay. Heavy artillery preparation followed the next day with the intention of cutting the German wire; trench mortars and rifle grenades were concentrated on the same task and at night machine-gunners ensured that gaps could not be repaired. On 27 June, Battalion and Brigade HQs moved up to "Mechanics" in the evening. After a two hour barrage the raid was made by 100 men of the 19th. London under cover of gas and smoke. The 20th. provided control posts at trench junctions. The raiding party entered the German front line to find that the gas had drifted northwards and not affected the defending troops. They bombed dugouts and did as much damage as possible before returning with one wounded prisoner. The German artillery remained quiet.

Two quiet days followed; the battalion and brigade HQs returned to Bully-Grenay on 28 June and on the 29th the 20th. went forward once more to the front line with the 23rd. London on their left and 140 Brigade on their right. A company of Nelson Battalion, of the R.N. Division was attached under instruction in front line duties and found the trenches very muddy and in places full of water. The month closed with the German artillery slightly more active and both sides busy with rifle grenades and trench mortars while working parties struggled to reconstruct the damaged trenches.

No. 143 **1 June 1916**

Dearest,

Thanks so much for your letter of Sunday last and for the parcel. We are still "resting". It is like our usual "rests" with plenty of work but it is indeed good to be out of that inferno for a while. The weather is grand and there is a prospect of a swim too. There is a swimming bath here which the engineers have almost completed. The water supply is a stream from the hills which runs in at one end and out of the other. The water is icily cold but should be very refreshing on a scorching hot day. Yesterday was market day here and the little town, especially the market square, was crowded with French people from round about.

I had intended, on Sunday next to go over to see Madame and the little boys where Bob and I were billeted once but I shall have to postpone it as I have just had a message from Will Pike that he is coming to tea that day. I shall be pleased to see him and have a chat with him. I had a letter from Storch yesterday and in it he says he saw you, or at least he thought he did, one day in a train coming from Cannon Street at about 6p.m. He said he recognised you from your photo and moreover you had a small 20th. badge on your collar and a number of green envelopes were sticking out of your bag. He was in "civvies" and sat directly opposite you in a 2nd class carriage. Do you remember the incident? I should very much have liked to have been with you at West Wickham.

Please give my congratulations to Charlie and Edith [on their engagement – Ed.].

I am so grieved to know that things are not going smoothly with you at home again. I do feel so sorry for you, my dear, and I feel so powerless to do anything for you, which seems to make it worse.

How can I comfort you? Would that I could take you away to a little home of our own. Where we could be so happy together; but that cannot be just yet.

You know that you have my love always. Try and let that fact comfort you for a bit. One day, dearest, we will be so happy and until then "au revoir".

Yours ever, Ted

P.S. This is quite a secret. I have heard it quite by accident. Do not tell anybody or mention it in a letter to me but I have been recommended for a DCM for a little job – nothing at all really – on that Sunday Evening. I have only told you and it probably won't come to anything so please say "nuffin".

Footnote to No. 143:
The award of the Military Medal to 1393 Sergeant E. H. Trafford was announced in the *London Gazette* on 14 September 1916.

No. 144 — Sunday evening 4 June 1916

Thanks for yours of the 1st. I am not surprised, really, that you did not hear much from me during that week 20th–27th although I sent you and Mother a Field card each day. We are still at the place from which I wrote last and have had a swim yesterday and today. The weather is not so hot as it has been, but it is still fine.

I walked over to R . . . . [Rimbert] yesterday to our old billet. Madame was pleased to see me and the little boys were wildly excited.

Will Pike has been over to tea with me today and we had a nice walk and "jaw" together.

I hope your dream will soon come true and that I shall really come home if only for a short leave. It should not be so very long now before I am home again, but do not begin to expect me just yet.

There is very little to write about and I do not feel in a writing mood tonight.

You know I love you all the time.

Good-night, darling. Yours ever, Ted

No. 145 — 10 June 1916

Thanks for your letter of the 6th. We are still back here and not having too hard a time. I saw Will Pike again on Thursday evening. He sent his kindest regards to you and your Dad. Yes, I did have a good time with him on Sunday. I forgot to mention that before. We had a nice long walk and then sat chatting over a bottle of champagne when I went back part of the way to the village where he "lives". The weather is not as good as it might be at this time. There is a lot of rain about and it is not very hot. The swimming bath therefore which is a very cold one and in the open air, of course, is not as attractive as it might be. I have been doing a little reading this week and now I have finished "The Edge O'beyond". I think I can confirm my original opinion, expressed in my last letter, that it is a good book, but that it does not appeal very strongly to me. I have also read "The World's Desire" by Rider Haggard. This is a very good book and Sonny has promised me "A Knight on Wheels" by Ian Hay. Have you read either?

We had a concert last night in a hall which was once a barn or some such place, but which has been converted into a nice little concert hall. It was here that we went to the pictures the other evening. I sang a Scotch song and helped in a little comic affair. The whole affair was quite a success with footlights and a nice little stage.

I have not seen the article you refer to, in the "Chronicle". I should like to. Will you send it out? I will return it again.

Was not the news of Lord Kitchener's death a thunderbolt? We all laughed at the rumour at first and were staggered when the truth came out. It seems as if we are an unlucky lot. One catastrophe after another; but still the Naval affair seems better now, although the losses were so tremendous. The Russian news is more cheering.

I think I have not much more to talk about. You know all I would say. I should like to tell you all I cannot write. I want you all the time.

I am glad you write to your cousin Jack. Of course I don't mind. If my girlie

Footnotes to No. 145:

1 Lord Kitchener lost his life when *H.M.S. Hampshire* was sunk on 5 June 1916.

2 The battle of Jutland was fought on 31 May 1916. The British losses included three battle-cruisers: *Queen Mary*, *Indefatigable* and *Invincible*, and three cruisers: *Defence*, *Black Prince* and *Warrior*.

can't write to her own cousin who is also a lonely soldier, she must have a fickle fancy.

Do you think it would make me jealous? Not a bit of it! You love me too well for me to get into a flurry over a few letters. I know you are mine, dearest, and that I am yours.

With all my love, Ted

P.S. We are on the move again.

No. 146 **13 June 1916**

Many thanks for your letter of the 9th and also for the parcel which arrived with it.

Our post has been delayed for some days and we had quite a collection of parcels in the mess. One man had some kippers in his and we had such a meal for tea! Kippers followed by homemade black-currant jam and your excellent cake and chocolates.

You will be surprised to know that our brigade is in the line again, but this battalion is not in the trenches at present. Instead we are in billets just behind the line and go up on carrying parties each night. The weather has been awful again, cold and wet. The day I wrote last it poured, and since, each day has been a thorough soaker. It looks as if I shall have a wet journey tonight. We left the place we were at on Sunday and completed the first part of our journey by train and a short march, which took place in an awful storm which wet us all through. We spent Sunday night in huts where we have been before and where the woods were so beautiful [Verdrel]. We left there on Monday and had another wet journey to here [Sains-en-Gohelle – Fosse 10]. We are billeted fairly comfortably in a cottage and sleep on the floor, something of a change after the bed, especially as we have no blankets now, because the calendar shows it to be warm(?)

I am reading now, "The Vultures" by H. Seton Marriman. It is a good book about Diplomacy & Secret Service Agents.

Thanks for the 'phone number. I hope I shall soon be in the happy situation to be able to use it, but I am afraid it is not just yet.

"Sonny" will probably be leaving us soon as he has been offered and accepted a commission in this battalion.

I had a letter today from Sergt. Hicks' mother. She says he has been dangerously ill. She was wired for, to come and see him in hospital in Northampton. He had a double fracture of the knee and has had several operations. Did I tell you that another of my pals was killed in that affair at Vimy? Sergt. Francis Carter. He was a fine chap and we miss him a lot in the mess.

I must close now, my dearest, so once more, au revoir, with all my love.

Yours ever, Ted

No. 147 **17 June 1916**

It is Sunday and I have not yet replied to your last Sunday's letter. Thanks very much for it and the subsequent one of the 14th also thanks for "Punch". That is jolly good this week. We are still where I wrote from last and by the way the prophecy about getting wet was quite correct. I was wetter that night than I have ever been. Every mortal thing I had on was soaked through. I am still quite fit however, and I trust you are too. Last night was fearfully moonlight and I don't know whether you have seen Bairnsfather's drawing where the girl at home looks out and says "To think that the same old moon is shining down on him"; while he is wiring in front of the trench and looking savagely at the moon, saying "That . . . . . . moon will be the death of me". We were in that state, working out between the lines, ours and the Bosch, hoping that something would cloud the moon over for a bit.

The weather generally has improved and is fairly summery again, and we have now the Daylight Savings Bill in effect. It seems peculiar that it is light until 10 o'clock nowadays.

Thanks for your cousin Jack's letter. It is really very "Yankee" and to get the full effect should be read with a "twang". I think all the Canadian troops think that they are coming out to finish the War; of course I know he only said what he did in fun. I wish they would do the same with us as the papers say they are doing with some "Anzacs" out here, who were given a week in England, because they did a bit of good work out here. Such privileges seem only to fall to the well paid Colonial troops and I tell you they don't become any more popular with our boys when they read such things as that. Don't take this seriously. It's only a little growl.

You say I don't tell you enough about my pals. Well we have a mess of 6 now – "Sonny", CQMS "Bobs", Sergt. Barker who was I think a pal of Charlie (he was then a lance corporal), Sergt. Machen a very nice fellow from Plumstead and an old school pal of Mallet (that's strange isn't it?) and Sergt. Wiltshire a rather slow sort of chap.

We all get on well together and have quite jolly little times together when we get a chance.

Who do you think I have run across in this village? Will James again! He is quite well and sends kindest regards.

Fancy Crowley being in the R.N.D.! Does he expect to come out here?

If you missed a letter I suppose you got no information about the pictures. "John" and "Jim" in one of them, the two brothers, and "Jim" did them. Both were wounded on the same day. In the group we are outside our billet. Don't you think it looks cosy?

You guessed my Scotch song rightly, or did you know that was the only one I knew?

Footnote to No. 147:
17 June was actually Saturday and not Sunday as Ted says at the beginning of his letter.

Glad to hear you are looking after yourself a bit. I do hope the "beastly" cold is better now.

That's all for now. I want you more than ever and still no immediate prospects of leave. Still, hope on. I might be lucky soon.

With all my love. Yours ever, sweetheart, Ted

P.S. Only just discovered the cutting. Thanks!

"The same old moon."

See Letter No. 147

From *Fragments from France* – Bruce Bairnsfather.

No. 148 — 20 June 1916

Thanks for your letter of 17th June. We are still where I last wrote from and are not having too bad a time. I am quite well and trust you are now.

Yes, Sonny is leaving today to attend a Cadet School where he will be gazetted as an officer in this battalion. I shall again be acting CSM. It is a shame though to lose all one's pals like this.

There was an investiture yesterday by the General when our chaps received decorations for the Vimy business. We had 3 military crosses (1 officer and 2 CSMs), 1 clasp to an officer who had already got a cross and who by the way is seriously wounded, 3 DCMs and 2 military medals.

Our company did not get anything at all.

Poor old Hicks has had his leg amputated. It seems terrible to think of and out here won't bear thinking of much.

I hope your new hat and dress won't be out of fashion by the time I get leave again.

We have a cricket match on tomorrow. Sergeants v Officers. I hope it keeps fine and the place doesn't get shelled. The Bosch in the observation balloon will see a good match for nothing.

So Stan is home at last. He must feel "bucked". I should feel like dancing on my head I think, so look out for a maniac if I do get leave soon.

That's all, I think for the present. You know how much I want you. We will be so happy one day, my darling.

With all my love, Yours ever, Ted

No. 149 — 22 June 1916

Thanks for your letter of Monday. As you see, we are in the line, but we are not having too bad a time. The weather is quite hot and the flies are becoming rather a pest. The trenches we are now in are quite picturesque. All around, except for patches of brown earth shell holes, is gay with poppies and other brilliant weeds and wild flowers.

There seems to have been quite a procession in our road on Sunday evening but I should have liked the opportunity of being able to join in and make it a bit bigger.

I am having quite a busy time but I am quite well looked after really. The CSM you know! I get jolly good rations sent up and I have a peach of a chap to look after me, cook etc.

I had a mutton chop and fried potatoes for dinner today.

Thank Alec for kind regards and give him mine, if you get the chance. I am still quite well.

There seems so little now to write about, but I knew you would like a letter even if there was nothing in it.

You know how eagerly I look forward to seeing you. I want to just be with you, that's all.

With all my love, Yours ever, Ted

The "peach" is a fat man of about 35, known as "Bunny".

Footnote to No. 149:
"Bunny" was a familiar figure during the author's childhood, regularly walking past the family home in Humber Road, Blackhealth.

JULY 1916

On 1 July the Nelson Battalion, the Royal Naval Division relieved the 22nd. London and the following day the Naval Company which had been attached to the 20th. took over a portion of the front line but remained temporarily under the orders of the Commanding Officer of the 20th. The next day 141 Bde. was withdrawn to divisional reserve on its relief by 142 Bde. The 23rd. London took over the front from the 20th. which moved off by half platoons back to Fosse 10 south of Sains-en-Gohelle.

A draft of two hundred men arrived on 4 July; the battalion bathed and the armourer sergeant inspected all rifles. The new draft plus all officers and NCOs not on duty marched to Sains-en-Gohelle the next morning for a farewell parade and inspection by Brigadier General Thwaites who that day left 141 Bde. on promotion to Major General to command 46th. Division. For three nights large working parties (387 men on 5 July and 200 on each of the following nights) carried stores and ammunition from Aix-Noulette to the front line; by day the German artillery was shelling the British battery positions in front of the town. Captain Goodwin left the battalion to take up post as Town Major of Pernes.

The 20th. handed over their billets on the evening of 7 July to the 7th. London and later the same night moved into accommodation vacated by the 8th. London in Noulette Wood. Six days of busy "relaxation" followed during which one officer and 100 men joined the battalion from base. This was a period of intense training which included firing on the ranges, gas helmet drill, signalling by Very Light and by rocket, wire cutting by the new "Bangalore Torpedo" and scouting and intelligence work. The latter was covered by a lecture to officers at Hersin on 9 July. Night working parties assisted the Royal Engineers in carrying up supplies, in cleaning and repairing dugouts and in manning a water control post. The whole battalion bathed on 12 July and spare time activities included evening cricket matches and a voluntary Church Service in the recreation hut on Sunday 9th. At 01.30 on 10 July a salvo of shells burst in the valley behind Noulette Wood and the batteries on both sides of the wood were shelled.

The period from 13–19 July found the 20th. back in the trenches again – this time in the Souchez left sub-sector. Taking over from the Drake Batt. of the Royal Naval Division, and holding a section of line between 21st. London on their left and 18th. London on their right. 'B', 'C' and 'D' Coys. were in the front line with 'A' Coy. in reserve in front of Noulette Wood. Captain Webb (18th. London) was appointed temporary second in command of the 20th. This proved to be an eventful week which cost the

20th. thirty-four casualties. On 14 July the 141 Bde. Trench Mortars strafed the enemy lines during the morning and the German retaliation in the afternoon came in the form of a bombardment of the London support positions with 5.9s trench mortars and "minnies", to which our artillery replied. In the evening a patrol from the 17th. London was caught by enemy rifle grenades when returning to our lines at the double block at the end of "Rotten Row" trench. A company of the Hood Batt. of the Royal Naval Division was attached to the 20th. for that night for trench warfare experience. The morning and afternoon pattern of tit-for-tat trench warfare was repeated the next day when several casualties were suffered (including 2nd Lieutenant White severely wounded) and the trenches badly damaged; the latter called for a busy night's repair work in addition to heavy duties for the usual carrying parties. Fifty men from 'A' Coy. came up to the front during the night as reinforcements, led by Captain Read who had escorted forty men from 'B' and 'D' Coys. out to Noulette Wood. In the course of the afternoon of 16 July in heavy bombardments our artillery cut the enemy wire and then in the evening registered on the communication trenches. The expected German retaliation came in the form of 5.9s. Our guns opened up again at 01.00 hours the following morning for forty minutes, then 2nd Lieutenants Borrodaile and Halford led eighty-six men of the 20th. in a raid on the enemy front line; this provoked only minor retaliation and no Very Lights were put up. 2nd. Lieutenant Borrodaile was badly wounded in this action; one man was missing and seventeen slightly wounded. In the afternoon the 20th. trenches were badly damaged again by "minnies" calling for further repair work after dark; a night patrol sent out in the hope of taking a prisoner, returned without making contact with the enemy. Reconstruction of trenches continued all day on 18th July – the day on which Captain Kershaw of the 19th. London joined the 20th. as temporary second in command.

For the 20th., their last day in the line before rest and retraining to take part in the Somme offensive, was a long one. At 02.15 hours 19 July, 2nd Lieutenant Flanigan and a twelve man patrol went out after two 2 minute bursts of trench mortar and artillery fire ten minutes apart. They found a large working party in the German front line and decided not to attempt to attack them. The battalion was relieved at midnight 19/20 July by the Hawke Battalion of the Royal Naval Division and marched back to Fosse 10 near Sains-en-Gohelle into divisional reserve, where it was strengthened by the arrival that day of two junior officers (Boxall and Steel) and 183 men from base. The Brigade Commander inspected the battalion the next day at the rear of the chateau at Sains and the same location the following day saw a Church Parade. All men were able to bath at the pithead baths and then at night came the now familiar carrying parties to transport gas cylinders from "Colonel's House" to the trenches in the Angres sector. Three days of training and assimilation of the replacements followed and inspections of rifles by the Armourer Sergeant and of boots by the Sergeant Master Shoemaker, combined with one last night's work carrying up cylinders from Corons d'Aix.

On 27 July 141 Brigade moved off from the Arras-Béthune area where it had spent more than a year, the 20th. marching from Hersin to new billets in Camblain Chatelain. It was a very hot day and several men fell out – possibly because of the recent changes of boots. Two days of marching, drilling and bayonet fighting practice followed before the next move, on 30 July, via Ourton south westwards to Ternas; despite the heat only three men from the battalion fell out on this march.

No. 150 **3 July 1916**

Came 'out' today. Will write a long letter tomorrow. Am quite well. Thanks for letter of 30th.

Au revoir, Yours, EHT

No. 151 **5 July 1916**

I must apologise for not writing, as promised yesterday, but I have been so busy with so many things after such a time in the line, when books etc. get a bit behind. Yesterday evening my promotion to CSM was a feature of the orders, so now, if you please, I wear a crown in lieu of stripes. I have not heard from Sonny again so I do not know whether he received Elsie Smith's letter or not.

I heard some very bad news today; that Jack Hicks had died. Another pal gone for good! I feel so sorry for his people. He was the only son and they almost worshipped him.

Our last turn in was not too bad so long as it kept fine but one day we had a violent thunderstorm and how it rained! I was in a dugout one entrance of which happened to be situate in the lowest part of the trench. The opening served as a splendid drain to about 50yds. of trench and we had a splendid game of sewer rats.

It was funny to see the water pouring in and things floating round, while "Bunny" and I paddled about rescuing them. We finally got an old pump (used for clearing trenches of water) which squirted water all over and a length of very defective hose which, when patched up with sandbags, gave a fine "Heath Robinson" effect and after much fixing and adjusting we got most of the liquid mud out. We had some exciting times in that dugout.

We also made a raid on the Boche (sic) lines. I was not one of the party that went over but those that went did a lot of damage and had very few casualties. I have seen the second edition of "Bairnsfather" but do not think they are as good as the first. They seem to be "made to order" rather than "inspired".

You talk about young Landon being a kid to be an officer. I could tell you a thing or two about boy officers of whom I have had experience.

I have now quite a decent billet where I and the CQMS share a bed but I suppose it is only for a day or two. The only drawback is that it is the end house of the village and the fields adjoining are full of guns the crash of which nearly shook us out of bed one night, but thank goodness they have been fairly quiet except on that one occasion. I saw Will Pike in the line, he was quite well the day we came out. He was one of the men who threw smoke bombs for our raid. He sends kindest regards.

Would you please, next time you are at our place get hold of my fountain pen, it is a Watermans "Ideal", and send it to me, together with some ink pellets which I think can be obtained at Boots. A pen would be useful to me now. There is one other thing which is very useful (I have usually borrowed one before) and that is a "Primus" stove, but they are rather expensive. Should you feel extravagant tho', they can be obtained at Selfridge's. These stoves are an absolute boon and I can obtain the oil from our QM Stores. You always want to know what I want.

I hope you and yours are all quite well. Give my kindest regards to your Dad.

I am wanting you all the time, darling, but leave has again been stopped. I only hope the post is not stopped, as rumoured. Don't you think the last picture in the 2nd "Fragments" is good?

Au revoir, sweetheart. With all my love, Ted

No. 152 — 8 July 1916

Thanks so much for nice long letter of the 4th. You can guess how glad I was to get it, the two previous ones were quite short ones, weren't they?

You will think me greedy to always expect long ones when I don't write very long ones myself. I have heard of "Action Front" but have never read it. I have just started "The Rocks of Valpré" by Edith M Dell. It seems all right.

You had quite a good time with Elsie Smith. As you say you always do and by the way that reminds me that Bob owes me a letter.

Sorry to hear that your little watch had gone wrong. Is it alright now? Mine went wrong a little while ago and I took it to a French watchmaker, while we were back resting, but it stopped again about a fortnight ago and remained stopped for some days when it suddenly started all on its own and has gone since quite well.

You say that you feel more lonely on Sundays, so do I, but Sundays are like every other day so you see, as far as you are concerned I am always lonely. I do want you so but once more "Au revoir".

With all my love, Yours ever, Ted

No. 153 — 12 July 1916

Thanks for your letters of the 4th and 6th, and for the parcel. Those little cocoanut cakes are really delicious.

We are still where I wrote from last but expect to be in the line again soon. There is not much in the way of news to tell you. I am still quite busy. In fact it seems as if I shall always be so, but then the time goes quicker like that. The weather which after the wet spell became quite summery has again broken and it is quite chilly now especially at nights. I will write you a really nice long letter soon but this I am afraid must be quite a short one. You know all I would say. I want you always and I think constantly of you. I trust you and yours are all well. Thanks for Jack's letter. Once more, my love, au revoir, with all my love.

Yours ever, Ted

No. 154 — 21 July 1916

You will begin to wonder where this letter has got to, but you must know that the field cards are, at the time, all I can send, and even in them, unsentimental and stereotyped as they are, I hope you can read the message of love I invariably send with them. Thanks so much for the little stove which has just arrived. Don't you think they are jolly little chaps? We are out of the line and I am at the billet where I had a bed last time so am comfortable again. Thanks also for the pen and for "Punch" etc. In fact, thanks for all you have ever sent me. By the way, what joke was it you were playing when you sent me a year old "Kentish Mercury" with some very stale news in it? I did keep the heading but I have now lost it. It was dated 18 June 1915. Was there anything important in it or can it be that it took a year to reach me? I lost the wrapper. We had a photograph taken today so I hope to send a copy of that in a day or two. You ask me about the pay; it is what you suggest, so I ought to get a credit balance after a little time, but I am afraid we are a bit extravagant when we get a chance to be and the smallest luxury is about twice the price what it is in England. I don't wish to raise false hopes, but there is a likelihood of leave starting again in September. Wouldn't it be just perfect if it happened during your holiday and I were lucky!

So your cousin Jack has got out here. Let me have news of him. He is certainly keen.

I seem fairly lucky with my post, my letters arrive fairly regularly but some of the other chaps get them horribly delayed.

The weather seems to have made a change for the better at last and we can now believe that it is summer. I am still quite well and I hope that you are too. How is your Dad? Please give him my kindest. I have not seen Will Pike lately but he is quite well, I had a message from him today. He is now a sergeant.

Glad that your aunt, of whom I know you are fond, was with you for a bit. Thank her when you write for her kind regards which are reciprocated.

Fancy Don Thatcher a cadet! I suppose he gets a bit longer in England that way. He might have got included in a draft if he stayed in the 3rd. and that would never do. I heard of Les Howard the other day, but I don't keep up a correspondence with him. He has at last joined up. I shouldn't like to head my letters "Derby" and it is not a case of "the fox who lost his tail". If many of the willing Derbyites had joined up a few months earlier the whole job would never have been so hard and the end would have been nearer. However that's not what I want to write about.

I want to tell you how much the thought of my own dear girlie waiting so patiently and bravely for me, is. I tell you it is a great incentive to know that there is that "someone" who cares so deeply and who appreciates.

Darling, a pen can never express all I would tell you. I am just burning to take you in a loving embrace and kiss away all your fears. How happy I know we could be! Just a little longer. Just a few more weary weeks of waiting and we'll be so happy together.

Just you and I, think darling – I am happy in spite of all to know, not the depth of your love, that is impossible, but that there is such love for me.

Good night sweetheart. Yours, Ted

P.S. Excuse the muddle of the pages but I started to economise after the 2nd page.

'B' Coy. Sergeants' Mess 21 July 1916. 20th. London Regiment.
L. to R. (back) Pinder, Keeble, Stevens, Burley, Hogg
(front) Machen, Roberts, Trafford, Barker, Wiltshire
See Letter No. 155

No. 155 **24 July 1916**

Thanks so much for your letter of the 19th. I am always glad to get your letters. What do you think of the enclosed? Sonny is still away from us. I have written him today. I expect he will soon be back with us again. Fancy Charlie going to the office again! I expect he found the change a strange one.

There is little to write about so I will just run thro' the sergeants in the photograph. Taking them from left to right. Sergt. Pinder is a new sergeant and quite a decent chap. Sergt. Keeble or "Pinkie" was a friend of Charlie. He was a private then. In the centre is "Bunny" Stevens of whom I have already told you. Then Burley who was a corporal in the military police. Sergt. Hogg is a very nice chap, recently a corporal in the bombers. Then the front row, Freddie Machen is the one I like best. He went to school with Mallet and was a great friend of Hicks. "Bobs" or Roberts is the CQMS and it is with him I have been sharing a bed. Sergeant Barker was also a pal of Charlie and is a good chap. Wiltshire at the end is a funny fellow, I have never quite got to the bottom him. There are two others. One of them, Sergt. Moore late of the bombers and a pal of Hogg, is a very nice chap.

That's all at the present. Au revoir my dear.

With all my love. Yours ever, Ted

No. 156 [Camblain Chatelain] **30 July 1916**

Thanks very much for your letter of 23rd. It is just a week since it was written and I got it yesterday. Our posts are getting quite irregular and for the last few days we have been unable to send off letters owing to being on "trek".

We have a big march today and did another two days ago. We seem to be on a walking tour through France but the weather is really too hot for us to appreciate it. The country is beautiful. At the last place we stayed two days and I had a fine billet, but the place we are at now is quite void of accommodation. My billet is like Bairnsfather's "Farm", no doors, no windows, but the weather is fine and warm for sleeping. Were it not for the heavy dews I should sleep in the fields.

There is not a lot more to write about. I am wonderfully fit although some of the chaps seem a bit knocked up. I hope you are quite well and your Dad.

Give him and your friends my kindest regards.

With all my love, Yours ever, Ted

AUGUST 1916

The 47th. Division spent August right out of the battle zone in intensive re-training in preparation for the part it was to play in the later phases of the Somme offensive. During the first half of the month 141 Bde. was centred on St. Riquier, the 20th. being billeted in the village of Agenvillers which had been reached in three days marching from Ternas. On the way the way the battalion had bivouacked in fields and orchards at Bonnières and Maison Ponthieu.

On 8 August came the announcement that 2nd Lieutenant Borrodaile had been awarded the M.C. for his exploits in the Angres sector during July. A three day Brigade Exercise held in Crécy Forest from 15–17 August rekindled the spirit of victory in the men of the 20th. nearly five hundred years after the famous battle of Crécy.

The march back towards Albert – the hub of the Somme front – commenced on 20 August, the 20th. making night halts at Ailly-le Haut Clocher, Flesselles and Molliens-au-Bois before reaching Brèsle, where the whole battalion is said to have been billeted in one large wooden hut. More training was carried out; a bathing parade at Heilly on 26 August; and on the last day of the month a Brigade Exercise involving cooperation with an aeroplane. That night a working party of one officer and one hundred other ranks laboured at the ammunition railhead at Edgehill.

No. 157 **2 August 1916**

Dearest,

Do you realise that it is just two years ago today that on the eventful Sunday morning we went joyously off to camp. And what years they have been?

I am writing this in idyllic surroundings. If this were just a holiday picnic and you too were here it would be ideal. We are bivouacking in a charming orchard surrounded by huge tall trees which afford shade all day long. We sleep at night under the stars; the weather being so warm that we have not troubled to rig up any shanties.

We are in a picturesque, old fashioned French farming village – a very sleepy place, where we can obtain a very decent home-brewed cider. The only drinkable stuff in the place. We came here yesterday. The weather was too hot to march but of course we can't choose the weather.

The night before last, before we left our last halting place, we had quite a gay evening, when we got through quite a lot of champagne and – "tell it not in Gath" – the officers of our company assisted us therein.

Did I acknowledge your letter of the 23rd? If not, thanks very much for it and the one of the 26th. It seems incredible that Harry Tate still does "Motoring". had he been out here when we first came he could have produced a fine farce on "Mortaring".

You had quite a good afternoon and evening on that day, hadn't you?

Fancy you running across Marion as you did. How is she? Should you see her again, please give her my kindest. I had expected another letter from you today, but I must not be greedy. The little "Primus" goes fine.

Well, I must soon close or miss the post and I know you don't want me to do either but I must be cruel to be kind, so once more au revoir.

With all my love, Yours ever, Ted

P.S. Shall think of you tonight as I lie on the grass looking at the stars thro' the trees. Good night.

No. 158 **5 August 1916**

Thanks for your letters of 27th and 29th, also for the parcel and the "Bystander". I think it is a really topping paper. The cucumber too was a pleasant change and I believe I prefer those little cakes to an ordinary one. Of course the tobacco was useful. Just lately I am glad to say the cigarettes have had a rest and the pipe has again come into its own. I am always thanking you for something but thank you, this time for the Kentish Mercury, which happened to be dated 1916.

It is quite a good idea to send your cousin a parcel. He, probably, is less fortunate than I am in privileges and opportunities to obtain little luxuries so send him a nice one instead of one to me one week.

So Charlie is going on garrison duty, presumably in England. When you write to him again, please give him my regards and tell him that his pal Voight is back with the Batt and has been made a lance corporal in 6 platoon – ink's run out – but am filled up again.

Have you decided yet about your holiday? How and where to spend it?

The weather is still splendid and to dodge the heat we start early in the morning. Yesterday we moved off from the orchard from which I wrote last and stayed last night in another similar place. We were up at 3 a.m. to get the march done before it got too hot. It turned quite chilly in the evening so we lit a big camp fire and sat round it in the twilight and darkness and sang all the songs we could think of. We were off again early this morning but did not do more than about 8 miles and here we are, in a dead and alive little village where my present billet is a hay loft in a huge, dirty farmyard where numbers of ducks hold noisy committee meetings all day and, I expect, all night too.

I'm glad you were so pleased with the photos and you think "Bunny" is misnamed. Perhaps so but he came with that name from the 3rd. Batt. and he says that when he first joined he supposes he was more like his namesake.

We are now quite a long way from "the line" but for how long one cannot hazard a guess. I think we are farther back than we have been before.

I have not yet read the book you sent but most of A. W. Mason's are. At least I liked his "Four Feathers" very much. Have you read that?

Now there is really not much more to tell you except that I am just longing for leave to start again so that, even for a short time I could see you again and tell you far more than I can write. Au revoir, my girlie.

With all my love, Yours ever, Ted

No. 159 — 7 August 1916

I had hoped for another letter today but for some reason or another we have no post today. However that makes it almost a "cert" for tomorrow, doesn't it?

What sort of a day have you had today? I understand that today's holiday has been entirely unrecognised as such. It has been here, as usual. We did spend a day in the country, starting at 6.30 this morning and returning after a field day at 4.30 this afternoon. The sun has been very powerful and my face is skinning with its effects. I feel quite fit and not very tired. I rarely get really tired now although I always sleep very well. Have you got any more socks finished yet? The army issue socks are rather hard and I get on much better with your nice soft woolly ones. One cannot have too many pairs when there is a lot of marching on the programme.

Speaking of programmes reminds me that we have not had a concert lately. It is time that a proper one was organised. We have little impromptu ones very often of course.

You will be sorry to hear that green envelopes are no longer issued – for the time being at least. I suppose some fools have violated the privilege and the stoppage is the result. It is much nicer to know that our little pen and ink conversations were only occasionally seen by others and then only by entire strangers.

I sincerely hope that you are quite well and that your Dad is too. There is much more I would like to say but I think you know pretty well what that is, so once more, au revoir.

With all my love, Yours ever, Ted

No. 160 — 10 August 1916

Thanks for your letters of 3rd and 6th. I am so sorry to hear of your aunt's continued annoyance and yet I am glad you have told me all about it. I may be able to comfort you a little. I know how miserable my girlie must be; I cannot tell you how I despise such a petty and mean temperament as your aunt seems to possess, but dearest do not take it too much to heart – remember that her outlook on life is very limited, that her views are very narrow and old fashioned. Add to these facts this, that she possesses a very spiteful and changeable nature and treat what she has to say with the contempt it deserves. I cannot understand a woman who does what she does to annoy you when you certainly deserve whatever consolation and comfort she is capable of. Perhaps, and I should rather think it is the case, she has never loved and does not understand anything deeper than a little fondness for a cat or a dog. Pity her shallow nature and please, my dear, for my sake, don't let it worry you too much. I am so angry when I think of it and I feel sure I could never be nice to her again.

I wish I could get a few minutes chat with Charlie. I think I understand him. Do you think if I wrote him a tactful letter I could improve the situation? Do let me do something to help you. I feel so helpless. I shall not worry more than I can help but I can't help – knowing and feeling how miserable you were when you wrote. But I know that by now things have smoothed down again and that you must feel better after having told me about it. I am going to ask the officer not to read this through but to take my word of honour as to its contents. I know he will do it so this is quite confidential.

My own girlie, I love you all the more when I know you are in trouble and need me more. Be brave, my dear, and one day I will and in our happiness we will forget together all these worries. Please don't ever refrain, for one moment, from telling me your troubles so that as far as possible we can share them. I have a broad back and can help you if in no other way than by the sheer strength of my love. I want you to be Oh so happy and let my love help to make you so even now.

I really think this is our trouble because I know my name is always mentioned but what do I care? It has also been mentioned by far more worthy persons than she.

I don't feel like writing about other things now, so once more a fond au revoir.

With all my strength I love you, Ted

P.S. Please tell Grace that they all send their love. I had to wait till Freddy was asleep to give him Grace's kiss and then had he been bigger I should have gone through it. It's the method of delivery that he objected to.

No. 161 — 14 August 1916

Thanks so much for your letter of the 8th. As you say it would be a jolly tour if we were together but I rather fancy I shall have lost the taste for open air cooking and living by the time I get back home. It gets a little tiny bit monotonous. What one wishes for is white linen and a nicely laid table. I am sure it would improve the food.

I do wish they would start again the issue of green envelopes; don't you.

You had quite a long jaunt with Grace. I know the little old fashioned shop and also I know the flavour of their ices.

We are having quite a stay at this place, from which I wrote last, but we have plenty of parades and field days. I am afraid the good weather has broken up. It is certainly cooler but we don't want rain, good as it is in some respects. We mortals are discontented beings; aren't we? When it's wet we want it dry and when it's hot we want it cold and so on in everything – we always want a change, except perhaps in one direction – I always want you and your love. I always want to make you happy. I pray that one day I shall.

I dreamt that I saw you the other night and you laid an arm on mine. I can almost feel the touch now, and just as I turned toward you – oh! tantalising vision – you just disappeared. Thank goodness that that part was a dream only.

Give my kindest to your Dad.

You have all my love. Yours, Ted

No. 162 — 16 August 1916

I have received no further letter from you. For some reason we have had no post for three days. I hope the posts home are more regular.

Yesterday we had quite a downpour here, but today is fine again. We have made no further move.

I really do not know what on earth to write about. I cannot describe our training or any thing like that. If we are still here on Sunday next I shall get a pass and visit the neighbouring market town, quite a big place, about 10 kilometres distant. By the way I had a letter from Sonny yesterday (the only ones we got were those posted in France) and he is very fed up because he has been put into another battalion – the 4th. London. I think it is a shame because had he known he would not come back to us he would never have taken his commission.

How are you? I hope still well and your Dad too.

I am quite fit. Heaps of love.

Yours ever, Ted

No. 163 — 19 August 1916

Thanks so much for your letters of 11th and 13th. I got them both together yesterday evening. I also heard from Harry Sanders. He was finally rejected for military service after about ten tries (real tries I believe) to get in.

He told me that Fred Wills who has a commission in the West Kents was shot up in that wood and was the only officer left in his company.

We have been very busy and are on the move so shall have to write you a longer letter later.

For the present, au revoir. With all my love, Yours, Ted

P.S. After all I was unable to get this off yesterday. We have had a fairly tiresome but not very long march, and are now in a village very much like all the others we have recently been in. A very dead and alive place.

Love, Ted

No. 164 [Brèsle] 23 August 1916

It is a long while since I wrote last and I know well, how keenly you will be expecting this. We have been travelling again and it is difficult to get letters off when we do not stay in one place for more than one night or so.

At present we are in a village which is about the last word. It is dirty and small, boasts of no shops and is packed with troops. The whole battalion is billeted in one huge shed and the sleeping accommodation is on shelves or platforms arranged like huge bookshelves in three tiers, access to which is gained by means of a ladder. I and the quarter master sergeant were lucky enough to get a little stable or barn with a thick layer of hay on which to sleep and very comfortable it is too. Our mess is in a vault or drying chamber of a little brewery. We have a table and forms rigged up and it serves its purpose well.

We are still enjoying fine weather but it is not so hot as it has been except at midday.

There seems such a little one can put in a letter now that we have no green envelopes.

You know quite well all that I would tell you.

You suppose that I have heard from Elsie all about her visit to Scotland, but no! I have not had a line from her for a long, long time. (The pen has run dry.)

So you have decided on Littlehampton or at least near there. You will see some of the hills we climbed on route marches at Arundel Camp.

I think that is all I have to say, so au revoir my dear.

With all my love, Yours, Ted

P.S. I have not yet written to Charlie. What is his address? I don't think however that just at present I will say anything to him.

P.S.S. I want some socks badly.

No. 165 26 August 1916

Many thanks for your letter of Sunday last. I am glad that you were spending such a pleasant week-end with Elsie.

We are still at the place I wrote from last. It is about the dirtiest place we have yet been in. To say it is filthy is a mild description. We have had rather frequent heavy showers and the place is now like a quagmire. Goodness knows what it is like in the winter.

One of our few forms of amusement(?) here is to have a look round, from the outside only, at a prisoners' camp near here, where quite a lot of Germans seem to have quite a good time.

Last evening we had a concert in a big shed. It was quite a success except the seating, which in most cases was standing. After, we went out on night operations and got some more rain. We have the same exercises for tonight again.

The only advantage in these is that it is cooler at night and we thereby miss the heat of the day.

So Alec has at last been discharged. Well it was useless for him to remain in the army, wasn't it and for his own sake it is better.

I am afraid I shan't get this finished this evening so will continue tomorrow.

Sunday Evening

I have just received your letter of Wednesday. Needless to say I was pleased to get it. I am so sorry if I have not acknowledged your parcel. I have received them alright unless you have sent one without mentioning it in a letter, and I believe I have acknowledged each. Are you fairly sure that none of my letters have gone astray? Does there seem an unbridged gap in them? You know what I mean?

I should very much like to see your new coat. You seem to like it yourself. Don't you as a rule criticise your purchases and wish you had got something else?

I think I shall start writing to your holiday address next Wednesday. I do hope you will have a nice time. Don't worry too much. It's not good for you, you know.

It has been quite wet today, but we had a nice bath this morning in a village not far from here. It was the first proper one with hot water we have had for a long time. A bucket in the fields has been the substitute for some time past.

I lost another pal today. This time Fred Machen has gone to a Cadet School with a view to taking up a commission.

There seems very little more to tell you. I am looking forward as hard as ever I can to leave in a month or so. Another "joy week" when it does come off. There is a rumour that by then, (a month hence) leave will have restarted. You know how I hope it is true.

I must ring off now. I've got some wrecks of socks to darn, so au revoir.

With all my love, Yours ever, Ted

No. 166 **29 August 1916**

Thanks so much for the letter and parcel of 25th. The socks were just what I needed at the moment. We just got in yesterday afternoon after being out in the worst rainstorm I've seen for a long time and were wet to the skin, when the post, with your socks, arrived.

The centre of the village, known as "Leicester Square" was a pond nearly knee deep when we came through it. We were lucky to be able to get our things dry here. The same thing happened today again. We went out on manouvres (sic) and got thoroughly wet and now we are sitting about in all stages of undress while our clothes dry again. When it does rain here, by gum it does "some". So you went again to Pinner? I am sure you had a good time. You always do there don't you? I only hope you are getting better weather there than we have here. It seems to hang about for days underfoot and almost ever since we have been here our boots have not been properly dry.

I wish you every success in your committee job. The object of the society is certainly a good one. You must let me know how it goes. I am always most interested to hear of anything in which you take a part.

The little coconut cakes you made were voted to be "better than ever". They are naturally very popular with our sergeants. I do wish those beastly "Zeps" would not disturb your beauty sleep. Did they do very much damage? I do hope they have not paid you a second visit.

I had quite a long letter from Elsie, so after all she has not forgotten me. I know you have not and you can rest assured that I think constantly of you.

Au revoir, my girlie, with all my love, Yours, Ted

Footnote to No. 166:
On 24 August 1916 several Zeppelins raided the east and south-east coasts of England, one of them reaching the outskirts of London. Eight civilians were killed and many injured.

Left: Ted's Father – Edward Trafford, 1914. Metropolitan Police Reservist-Inspector.

Right: Pat's Father – Charles Randall, 1916. In British Red Cross Society Uniform.
See Letter No. 75.

SEPTEMBER 1916 – HIGH WOOD

The 20th. greeted September with a circular route march from Brèsle via Hénencourt, Millencourt and La Viéville back to the starting point. There was a Church Parade on 3 September and a brigade boxing competition the following day. The battalion took part in a divisional operations exercise on 6 September and then again supplied a fatigue party of one officer and one hundred men to the ammunition railhead at Edgehill on the eighth of the month. On the Sunday two days later a Church Parade was mounted behind the Officers' Lines in Brèsle; the battalion was now ready to return to the battle zone.

The move started on 11 September when the 20th. marched to the support area behind Lozenge Wood east of Albert. In the evening they moved forward by platoons at 200 yard intervals to relieve the 1st. South Wales Borderers in the wood, where they bivouacked. On the fourteenth they moved up to the north-east corner of Mametz Wood, taking over from the 17th. London who were thus released to go ahead to the firing line. By midnight the 20th. were lined up along the edge of Mametz Wood and ready to go. Each man carried a day's rations, 2 iron rations, 2 Mills bombs, 2 sandbags and either a pick or shovel behind the haversack on his back. Hot tea and rum were issued. From 01.00 hours the battalion moved forward by platoons in file and took up positions on open ground on the slope in front of High Wood (Bois des Foureaux). On their way up they passed three of the new "armoured cars" (now known as tanks) which were scheduled to make their debut in support of the infantry later that morning. No casualties were suffered in reaching these positions although there was artillery activity over High Wood itself.

The front line trench ran through the southern corner of High Wood and was held by the 17th. and 18th. London who had gone up a little earlier to relieve 142 Bde. The right half of the 47th. Division front was in the hands of 140 Bde. of which the Civil Service Rifles adjoined the 141 Bde. sector. Neighbouring troops on the left were from the 30th. Division. The 19th. and 20th. Battalions were lying out in the open as described – just short of the wood itself. At 04.45 hours the 20th. Battalion HQ moved up into the congested support line where all four battalion HQs operated from a single dugout. At 06.00 hours (15 September) the 17th. and 18th. Battalions tried to crawl forward to lie out in shell holes in front of the trench to enable the 19th. and 20th. to come in to take their places. But in the growing light of dawn, they were seen and fired on suffering heavy losses. The 19th. and 20th. Bns. moved up but found insufficient space in the trenches which the 17th. and 18th. had been unable to evacuate. Most lay down along the edge of the wood where they also lost heavily. At 06.10 hours two tanks moved forward into the wood; one stuck almost at once, in the torn undergrowth and tree stumps but was able to continue to use its Hotchkiss 6 pounder and machine guns effectively. The other manoeuvred clumsily along the German line and stuck there. Its crew later set fire to it and abandoned it.

06.20 hours was zero hour for the infantry attack but little progress was made initially although all four battalions of 141 Bde. were involved in the wood itself with the 15th. London along the right edge. From 11.00 hours an half hour artillery barrage was called down on to the left side of the wood, and when this lifted, Captain Read and two platoons of the 20th. got into the enemy trenches on the left while a party from the 18th. managed to do much the same on the right. There were casualities as the two parties bombed their way towards each, but eventually the remnant of the German garrison surrendered. High Wood was cleared of the enemy by 13.00 hours and Captain Read, gathering some men of all battalions, went forward and established a new line by digging in under fire about 100 yards beyond the wood. 'A' Company was sent to the right to assist in linking up with 140 Brigade but lost heavily in doing so.

During this action on 15 September 1916 the 20th. had heavy losses; 13 officers and 250 other ranks became casualties. 141 Brigade losses totalled 1,179 of all ranks, while the 47th. Divisional casualties exceeded 4,500 officers and men. The next day, Major General Barter, G.O.C. 47th Division was relieved of his command for "wanton waste of men". 141 Brigade was so disorganised that its survivors were formed temporarily into a composite battalion under the command of Lieutenant Colonel Norman of the 17th. London.

Many of the London dead were buried opposite the south-western edge of High Wood on the other side of the road from Longeuval to Martinpuich. The 141 Bde. Chaplain, the Rev. David Railton conducted many of the burials and his Union Jack used for these, draped the coffin of the Unknown Warrior when he was laid to rest in Westminster Abbey on 11 November 1920. After a solemn dedication the same flag was placed above the tomb of the Unknown Warrior in the Abbey in 1921.

Ted Trafford was wounded early in the advance on 15 September and four days later he was in hospital in a converted school in Birkenhead. His fighting war was over but he "soldiered on" and as a Warrant Officer I, was one of the 20th. Battalion contingent in the Victory March of the London Territorials in 1919.

No. 167 — 1 September 1916

Dearest,

I suppose that by the time you receive this, you will be starting your holiday. I hope the weather and everything else is as one would have it for a holiday.

We have had a little relaxation this evening in the way of a performance by our Divisional "Follies", a concert party of ten men all of whom are really first class performers. They are properly organised and travel around the division when we are out of the line.

It was a really topping two hours amusement, better than many peirrots (sic) in England. They have proper costumes and make up. The only thing at fault is the accommodation. The performance this evening was in a huge delapidated barn with an improvised stage and candle footlights, but under the circumstances it was very good. I met Will Pike there and he came back to our mess to supper. He sends his kindest regards. Thanks for your letter of the 27th. Did I acknowledge the "Kentish Mercury" and "Bystander"? Thanks very much.

I am glad you had a pleasant time at Pinner with Evelyn.

I am sending a couple of rather interesting postcards. The names have now to be cut out to comply with censorship rules. You will see that the figure of the Virgin [on the Church at Albert] is now knocked into a horizontal position. This leaning statue can be seen miles away and the country people – always superstitious – say that when it falls to the ground the Germans will be thoroughly beaten and the war come to an end. It has, however, been in this position for months.

I had a letter from Reg Waterfield yesterday! He was reminded that he had not written lately by seeing "The Battle of the . . . . ." on the pictures! He is awaiting the result of an appeal made for him by his firm.

It is getting late, so good-night.

With all my love, Yours ever, Ted

No. 168 — 3 September 1916

Sunday today and a day of rest. It is too, for a change. I do not know what to write about; the weather is alright, I'm alright, most things are alright. They'd be a lot better if I could get some leave. Don't you think so?

Elsie in her letter gave me a tip, that the Highlands of Scotland would be ideal for a honeymoon. Think of it. I can't help thinking over that.

Your nice long letter of the 30th has just arrived. needless to say I am pleased to get it. I quite agree that it should do you good – this holiday I mean. Do get some snapshots or something so that I can share it a bit. I do wish you had taken my old camera. I forgot clean all about it and I suppose it is too late now.

It was quite a long time ago that you saw Elsie Phillips before your little outing with her. I haven't seen Will James for a long time either.

Your cousins are spasmodic sort of people. First one pops off then another and now without warning Effie pops back. I remember her quite. Was not she one of the party on the river when Stan lost his cigarette case? Do you remember that? It must be five years ago. What a long time!

Don't think I was grumbling about the socks, when I said I had some wrecks to darn. It is not often I have to do that, thanks to you, but the marching knocked them out a bit.

I hope you are having a really nice time in some pretty little English cottage and really having a good rest. I only wish I could be with you but you must really make the very best of it and wait just a little longer.

Au revoir, dearest. Yours ever, Ted

No. 169 — 6 September 1916

I have not had a letter from you since yours of the 1st. I know you have written but we have had no post today and there certainly would have been one in that.

I suppose you got off alright on Saturday, despite all the work you had to do. One generally manages to somehow. We are having much better weather and I hope that you are having the same sort.

You do get hold of some news through your friends. I have told you in my letters as much as one can put, honourably, into a letter. I don't know how your friends get to know.

Yes, I wish so many of the "old" men of the battalion had not gone away. It is much nicer and helps along the road too, to have good old pals with you, who have shared all the rough and good times with one.

We are having another show by our concert party tonight. I shall certainly make an effort to go. They are worth seeing and we cannot get too much of that sort of amusement.

I wonder where you are now. You must write really full descriptions of your holiday so that I can partly share it with you. I am happy if I know you are and I really think that you should be in the quiet calm of the country after busy, wartime London. Even old London, I suppose, must seem a very very different place to the peace time city. I should like to see it anyhow.

I really cannot write. I can't seem to find anything to talk about. Au revoir, my dear, have as good a time as you can.

With all my love, Yours ever. Ted

P.S. I am quite well.

No. 170 — 9 September 1916

Still no post from you. I begin to realize how precious your letters are. I think I shall not send this off until I hear from you or at least I will delay posting until this evening, when we may have some post. I feel as if I cannot write until I hear.

Saturday Evening

I have been out this afternoon with C.Q.M.S. Roberts to . . . . . [Amiens] a large town some 20kms. from here. We travelled each way by lorry and when I got back I found yours of the 3rd with the little sprigs of heather. Thanks so much. I feel much better now. You did have a journey down! Fancy missing Gladys and the train, but all's well that ends well. The place as you describe it seems delightful. What a long walk you had! It is some while since you walked so far. I wish the same remark applied here.

It is getting late so good-night, my dear.

With all my love, Yours, Ted

Sunday Afternoon

It is so annoying but I found last evening that there is no outgoing post today so your letter must perforce be still further delayed. I am so sorry. You will be so disappointed. This will go off tomorrow after we reach our destination for we are to move again – hence the post trouble.

The place we visited yesterday was a fine place with electric cars, (by the way we had a ride for the novelty), restaurants, where in one we had a good meal.

The Cathedral too is worthy of mention. A splendid building not knocked about but well protected by sand bags in case. There were shops and crowds of people where one could forget the war for a little while. But I could not help wondering where my little girl was and what she was doing.

This afternoon we were to play a rugger match but our opponents the London Irish did not turn up. I saw Will Pike today in his billet. He is laid up with a sprained ankle and will probably go to hospital.

There is no post in again today. I do want another letter. I hope to get one tomorrow. Again au revoir.

All my love, Ted

No. 171 — 13 September 1916

At last, letters from home and yours of the 5th arrived yesterday. I am still well.

We are living in dugouts behind the line and I find myself with heaps to do.

We are undoubtedly to go into some scrap soon. More I cannot tell, but do not worry if for a day of two you do not hear, although I will try to write as often as possible. Don't worry too much there's a dear. I would not spoil your holiday for worlds but I promised to tell you all I could.

You had a nice walk to Littlehampton. Not a bad little place is it? But you only thought of bathing. I wish I had a chance to bathe. I love swimming and yet we never seem to get a chance like we did once. I am afraid you are a bit of coward when you admit that Gladys bathed and you only paddled. Perhaps you want someone to teach you to swim? I will one day.

The deck chair "stunt" sounds most inviting too. I think that is another of my failings or at least things over which my very laziness becomes enthusiastic.

Yes, a book is always welcome but not war stories, thanks. Glad to hear of the wreck of the Zeppelin. Dad saw it and so did Harry Sanders. Elsie only woke up when all London cheered.

Now dearest, I think there is no more to say except what I would always say and for preference, verbally and whispered close to your ear, that I always love you and want you.

With all my love, Yours ever, Ted

Footnote to No. 171:
Thirteen Zeppelins raided the eastern counties of England on 3 September; one attempting to reach London was brought down near Enfield by Lieutenant W. L. Robinson R.F.C. who was later awarded the Victoria Cross for this feat.

No. 172 — 15 September 1916

I have been admitted into hospital and am going on well. Wounded (quite slightly). I am being sent down to the base. I have received your letter dated . . . . Letter follows at first opportunity.

Ted

No. 173 — 17 September 1916

Since you received my field card, I do not doubt but that you have been wondering what has happened to me. I am now in a Base Hospital with a shrapnel wound in the foot. Nothing serious at all. A small shrapnel bullet has passed through my big toe. Entering through the nail and passing out through the ball. I expect to be in England in a day or two when no doubt you will be able to see me.

Much love, Yours, Ted

No. 174 **Tuesday 19 September 1916**

From 'B' Ward, Temple Road Military Hospital, Birkenhead

I hoped to be in England, on leave in September, but I am not on leave yet although in England. What do you think of a trip up here to see me? I may be here some weeks yet. I should like to see you, but it is a long and tiresome journey. However if you do not mind that, I don't think the extravagance would be inexcusable. I was hit at about 7 a.m. on Friday morning in High Wood, Somme, and walked or rather hobbled with a rifle as a crutch to a dressing station and from thence proceeded by ambulance and train to a base hospital which I reached at about 6 a.m. on Saturday morning. Here I was popped into bed – did you notice that – a bed, and stayed until 10 p.m. on Sunday when I was roused up and dressed for "blighty". We left there at about midnight and "char-a-banced" to Etaples where we boarded a train for Calais, arriving there at about 8 p.m. yesterday. From there we crossed to Dover and came right through to here, passing through London, of course.

It would have been fine to have been left somewhere in London. We got here this morning at about 3.30 and were conveyed in motor cars to the hospital. I think it is a V.A.D. place, because the gentlemen who helped us bath and so on were in the blue uniform or "civies" (sic). They were awfully nice to us. Needless to say I have slept nearly all today. The nurses too are very nice to us and are V.A. workers, except the sisters who are territorials.

My foot is going on well I think, although before I left France there was a sign of septic poisoning.

Now, my love, I shall tell you no more but wait until I see you to tell you all about everything.

With all my love, Yours ever, Ted

No. 175 **Sunday 24 September 1916**

I wonder if you will come today. I delayed writing in case you suddenly decide to come, but I hardly expect you today. Next week-end I suppose.

Very many thanks for your nice long letter of Friday. I suppose that you are now at Maidenhead. Well if you have weather like this you should have a good day today. I was up yesterday and got down into the yard on crutches. I am going strong but cannot yet put any weight on the right foot. I went to Church this morning with a sergeant of the Yorkshires. I went nearly a mile each way. It made my arms tired, but the foot seems no worse. This afternoon if no visitors turn up, which I think is likely (that they won't I mean) I am going in a motor to a lady's house to tea with a sergeant major of the Wilts. The hospital is in a school building and visitors can see us any day between 2 and 6. Local people need a pass but if anyone came from London they could get in or better still I could get out, during those hours. We wear grey flannel suits, not blue, white shirts and red ties, but the nurse who is awfully nice, got some soft collars for me and a black knitted tie, so I do not look too much like a pauper but unfortunately I have my hair cropped quite short. This was done when I did not anticipate a trip to Angleterre. I think, my dear, much as I would like to see you at once, that it would be better for you to travel with Dad and Mother. You could see me for four hours each day if you came from Friday to Sunday, but please let me know when you are coming. I expect to be away from here in a month or six weeks. The bone of my toe is undamaged but the nail is all smashed up and there is a big hole to heal.

The news about dear old "Sonny" is awful. I feel so upset. He was so nice and he wanted to meet you. He knew all about you so you can tell what a friend of mine he was. His sister and his parents thought worlds of him. It is a blow for them. I saw his name in the casualty list a few days ago but they had an 'F' in his initials instead of 'I' but I thought at the time that it was he they meant. I also saw that poor old Len Cope, you remember him don't you, was killed. It was in the same copy of the Mercury. He was his widowed mother's only child.

Give my kindest regards to Elsie Smith please. I expect to hear from Bob soon, now that he has my address. I think that for the present we will leave Arthur's wedding present. We will talk it over when you come up. Think of something and tell me what. We will certainly give something jointly.

I arrived here with absolutely no kit – not even a hat, but I am fitted up fairly well. What I have not got I borrow. That's all I think for today, so for just a little while au revoir.

I want you so much, I am so happy to know that you are coming to me soon, but the days seem to drag when I am looking forward so to one day when you will arrive.

All my love is yours, Ted

Left: 2908 Sgt. Hicks, J.M. 20th. London Regiment, died of wounds 29-6-16. Buried Plumstead Cemetery, Woolwich.

Right: Captain Guy Williams, 1915.
See: May 1915 Vimy Ridge.

No. 176 **27 September 1916**

Thanks for Monday's letter. I am surprised that you had not got the Sunday letter I wrote. The reason I had not written before that was that I half expected to hear from you to the effect that you would be coming up during the weekend, but I did not really expect you. When you do come it will take nearly an hour to reach here from Liverpool. Tram to the pier, ferry to Birkenhead Pier and tram to Prenton, which passes the end of Temple Road. How I shall look out for you on Friday! It seems as if that day will never come.

Had quite a nice time on Sunday afternoon at a beautiful house with a most charming old fashioned garden. On Monday we, that is a R.S.M. of the Wilts. and I, went to West Kirby in a car he had hired. We had a lovely drive along the front and round the country. About 25 miles without walking a step. Yesterday I went on the car (democratic tram) to see Harry Sanders' aunt but only found his cousin at home. She and I had tea together and I was invited to come again. They have a very nice house, but I felt very shy. Glad you had such a nice time at Maidenhead. I am afraid all the summery weather will be gone before I get out. I am just longing to see you. Thanks for the congrats. I know nothing of this yet, not even whether it is a medal or a cross. You might bring a ribbon of whatever it is to put on my jacket.

Until Friday, then, a loving au revoir.

Yours ever, Ted

P.S. Am surprised but not in the least shocked at your fearful disclosure. I can't quite imagine you smoking somehow. I could Nellie or Effie. You did not say whether you liked it or not but you seemed very glad that there were no ill effects. You are quite proud of that ar'n't (sic) you?

No. 177 **3 October 1916**

I have been wondering what your feelings are. You have gone away again and those precious "little whiles" which I had <u>lived</u> for for so long are now but more tender memories. It was good to see you and after such pleasant anticipation it was sweet to feel you once more in my arms and taste your almost sacred kisses.

I am more than happy in your love. Such love so patient and brave. I want you still more than ever. I know you are mine. Oh! May the day hasten when I shall take you to be even more strongly mine. I cannot say all I feel, but I think, and cannot think of your wistful grey eyes without knowing the depth of character and the affection. I am looking out for a letter from you so I hope I shall not be disappointed in the morning. Stan came as expected and we have had a nice time together.

Good night, dear. With all my love. Yours – all yours, Ted

EPILOGUE

In the period covered by this book (10 March 1915–15 September 1916), members of the 20th. London were awarded the following decorations:

Commander of the Order of St. Michael & St. George	One
Distinguished Service Order	Three
Military Cross	Seven
Distinguished Conduct Medal	Eleven
Military Medal	Nineteen
Croix de Guerre	Two

The original 1st./20th. London, some of whose history I have recounted, continued to distinguish itself on the Western front throughout the war. The 2nd./20th., formed in 1914, went to France in July 1916 and was in action on Vimy Ridge before being sent to Macedonia and Palestine. This battalion returned to France in July 1918 and was in the forefront of the British advance into Germany in the closing days of the war. The 3rd./20th. was created as a depot battalion to train recruits as replacements for the two battalions overseas.

Pat and Ted were married in St. Mary's, the Parish Church of Lewisham, on 6 January 1917. Ted, having been declared unfit for further active service overseas, became R.S.M. of the 3rd./20th. and continued in that post until demobilised in 1919. Two sons were born to Pat and Ted; at the outbreak of the Second War in 1939 Leo, the elder (named after Leo Shurly, killed at Loos) had already enlisted in the R.A.F.V.R. in which he served 1939–46, mostly in the Middle East, and Peter, who is responsible for this book, was a medical student at St. Thomas's Hospital. Later, he served in the R.A.M.C. from 1945–53.

"THEIR NAME LIVETH FOR EVERYMORE"

Under this title, the Book of Remembrance of the 20th. Battalion, the London Regiment, was published by the Regimental Old Comrades Association in 1930. It contains the names of 1,031 members who made the Supreme Sacrifice during the Great War. Ted Trafford contributed the foreword to the memorial volume as well as assisting a devoted committee in the collection and checking of information.